D0488684

Qualifications and Credit Framework (QCF)

AQ2013

LEVEL 4 DIPLOMA IN ACCOUNTING

TEXT

Option Paper:
Personal Tax
FA 2015

August 2015 Edition

For assessments from January 2016

Third edition August 2015
ISBN 9781 4727 2176 1

Previous edition
ISBN 9781 4727 0910 3

British Library Cataloguing-in-Publication Data
A catalogue record for this book is available from the British
Library

Published by
BPP Learning Media Ltd
BPP House
Aldine Place
London
W12 8AA

www.bpp.com/learningmedia

Printed in the United Kingdom by Martins of Berwick
Sea View Works
Spittal
Berwick-Upon-Tweed
TD15 1RS

CONTENTS

BPP note: Assessments under FA 2014 will cease to be available from 31 December 2015. Assessments under FA 2015 will be available from January 2016. This Text edition includes the provisions of FA 2015. Please ensure you check the date you intend to sit your assessment to ensure you are using the correct material.

A NOTE ABOUT COPYRIGHT

Dear Customer

What does the little © mean and why does it matter?

Your market-leading BPP books, course materials and e-learning materials do not write and update themselves. People write them on their own behalf or as employees of an organisation that invests in this activity. Copyright law protects their livelihoods. It does so by creating rights over the use of the content.

Breach of copyright is a form of theft – as well being a criminal offence in some jurisdictions, it is potentially a serious breach of professional ethics.

With current technology, things might seem a bit hazy but, basically, without the express permission of BPP Learning Media:

- Photocopying our materials is a breach of copyright

- Scanning, ripcasting or conversion of our digital materials into different file formats, uploading them to Facebook or emailing them to your friends is a breach of copyright

You can, of course, sell your books, in the form in which you have bought them – once you have finished with them. (Is this fair to your fellow students? We update for a reason). Please note the e-products are sold on a single user licence basis: we do not supply 'unlock' codes to people who have bought them secondhand.

And what about outside the UK? BPP Learning Media strives to make our materials available at prices students can afford by local printing arrangements, pricing policies and partnerships which are clearly listed on our website. A tiny minority ignore this and indulge in criminal activity by illegally photocopying our material or supporting organisations that do. If they act illegally and unethically in one area, can you really trust them?

BPP LEARNING MEDIA'S AAT MATERIALS

The AAT's assessments fall within the **Qualifications and Credit Framework** and most papers are assessed by way of an on demand **computer based assessment**. BPP Learning Media has invested heavily to ensure our materials are as relevant as possible for this method of assessment. In particular, our **suite of online resources** ensures that you are prepared for online testing by allowing you to practise numerous online tasks that are similar to the tasks you will encounter in the AAT's assessments.

Resources

The BPP range of resources comprises:

- **Texts**, covering all the knowledge and understanding needed by students, with numerous illustrations of 'how it works', practical examples and tasks for you to use to consolidate your learning. The majority of tasks within the texts have been written in an interactive style that reflects the style of the online tasks we anticipate the AAT will set. When you purchase a Text you are also granted free access to your Text content online.

- **Question Banks**, including additional learning questions plus the AAT's sample assessment(s) and a number of BPP full practice assessments. Full answers to all questions and assessments, prepared by BPP Learning Media Ltd, are included. Our question banks are provided free of charge online.

- **Passcards**, which are handy pocket-sized revision tools designed to fit in a handbag or briefcase to enable you to revise anywhere at anytime. All major points are covered in the Passcards which have been designed to assist you in consolidating knowledge.

- **Workbooks**, which have been designed to cover the units that are assessed by way of computer based project/case study. The workbooks contain many practical tasks to assist in the learning process and also a sample assessment or project to work through.

- **Lecturers' resources**, for units assessed by computer based assessments. These provide a further bank of tasks, answers and full practice assessments for classroom use, available separately only to lecturers whose colleges adopt BPP Learning Media material.

This Text for Personal Tax has been written specifically to ensure comprehensive yet concise coverage for the AAT's **AQ2013** learning outcomes and assessment criteria.

Each chapter contains:

- Clear, step by step explanation of the topic

- Logical progression and linking from one chapter to the next

- Numerous illustrations of 'how it works'

- Interactive tasks within the text of the chapter itself, with answers at the back of the book. The majority of these tasks have been written in the interactive form that students can expect to see in their real assessments

- Test Your Learning questions of varying complexity, again with answers supplied at the back of the book. The majority of these questions have been written in the interactive form that students can expect to see in their real assessments

The emphasis in all tasks and test questions is on the practical application of the skills acquired.

Supplements

From time to time we may need to publish supplementary materials to one of our titles. This can be for a variety of reasons, from a small change in the AAT unit guidance to new legislation coming into effect between editions.

You should check our supplements page regularly for anything that may affect your learning materials. All supplements are available free of charge on our supplements page on our website at:

www.bpp.com/about-bpp/aboutBPP/StudentInfo#q4

Customer feedback

If you have any comments about this book, please email nisarahmed@bpp.com or write to Nisar Ahmed, AAT Head of Programme, BPP Learning Media Ltd, BPP House, Aldine Place, London W12 8AA.

Any feedback we receive is taken into consideration when we periodically update our materials, including comments on style, depth and coverage of AAT standards.

In addition, although our products pass through strict technical checking and quality control processes, unfortunately errors may occasionally slip through when producing material to tight deadlines.

When we learn of an error in a batch of our printed materials, either from internal review processes or from customers using our materials, we want to make sure customers are made aware of this as soon as possible and the appropriate action is taken to minimise the impact on student learning.

As a result, when we become aware of any such errors we will:

1) Include details of the error and, if necessary, PDF prints of any revised pages under the related subject heading on our 'supplements' page at: //www.bpp.com/about-bpp/aboutBPP/StudentInfo#q4

2) Update the source files ahead of any further printing of the materials

3) Investigate the reason for the error and take appropriate action to minimise the risk of reoccurrence.

A NOTE ON TERMINOLOGY

The AAT AQ2013 standards and assessments use international terminology based on International Financial Reporting Standards (IFRSs). Although you may be familiar with UK terminology, you need to now know the equivalent international terminology for your assessments.

The following information is taken from an article on the AAT's website and compares IFRS terminology with UK GAAP terminology. It then goes on to describe the impact of IFRS terminology on students studying for each level of the AAT QCF qualification.

Note that since the article containing the information below was published, there have been changes made to some IFRSs. Therefore BPP Learning Media have updated the table and other information below to reflect these changes.

In particular, the primary performance statement under IFRSs which was formerly known as the 'income statement' or the 'statement of comprehensive income' is now called the 'statement of profit or loss' or the 'statement of profit or loss and other comprehensive income'.

What is the impact of IFRS terms on AAT assessments?

The list shown in the table that follows gives the 'translation' between UK GAAP and IFRS.

UK GAAP	IFRS
Final accounts	Financial statements
Trading and profit and loss account	**Statement of profit or loss (or statement of profit or loss and other comprehensive income)**
Turnover or Sales	Revenue or Sales Revenue
Sundry income	Other operating income
Interest payable	Finance costs
Sundry expenses	Other operating costs
Operating profit	Profit from operations
Net profit/loss	Profit/Loss for the year/period
Balance sheet	**Statement of financial position**
Fixed assets	Non-current assets
Net book value	Carrying amount
Tangible assets	Property, plant and equipment

UK GAAP	IFRS
Reducing balance depreciation	Diminishing balance depreciation
Depreciation/Depreciation expense(s)	Depreciation charge(s)
Stocks	Inventories
Trade debtors or Debtors	Trade receivables
Prepayments	Other receivables
Debtors and prepayments	Trade and other receivables
Cash at bank and in hand	Cash and cash equivalents
Trade creditors or Creditors	Trade payables
Accruals	Other payables
Creditors and accruals	Trade and other payables
Long-term liabilities	Non-current liabilities
Capital and reserves	Equity (limited companies)
Profit and loss balance	Retained earnings
Minority interest	Non-controlling interest
Cash flow statement	**Statement of cash flows**

This is certainly not a comprehensive list, which would run to several pages, but it does cover the main terms that you will come across in your studies and assessments. However, you won't need to know all of these in the early stages of your studies – some of the terms will not be used until you reach Level 4. For each level of the AAT qualification, the points to bear in mind are as follows:

Level 2 Certificate in Accounting

The IFRS terms do not impact greatly at this level. Make sure you are familiar with 'receivables' (also referred to as 'trade receivables'), 'payables' (also referred to as 'trade payables'), and 'inventories'. The terms sales ledger and purchases ledger – together with their control accounts – will continue to be used. Sometimes the control accounts might be called 'trade receivables control account' and 'trade payables control account'. The other term to be aware of is 'non-current asset' – this may be used in some assessments.

Level 3 Diploma in Accounting

At this level you need to be familiar with the term 'financial statements'. The financial statements comprise a 'statement of profit or loss' (previously known as an income statement), and a 'statement of financial position'. In the statement of profit or loss the term 'revenue' or 'sales revenue' takes the place of 'sales', and 'profit for the year' replaces 'net profit'. Other terms may be used in the statement of financial position – eg 'non-current assets' and 'carrying amount'. However, specialist limited company terms are not required at this level.

Level 4 Diploma in Accounting

At Level 4 a wider range of IFRS terms is needed, and in the case of Financial statements, are already in use – particularly those relating to limited companies. Note especially that a statement of profit or loss becomes a 'statement of profit or loss and other comprehensive income'.

Note: The information above was taken from an AAT article from the 'assessment news' area of the AAT website (www.aat.org.uk). However, it has been adapted by BPP Learning Media for changes in international terminology since the article was published.

ASSESSMENT STRATEGY

This unit will be assessed via a computer based test of two hour duration. The competency level is set at 70%.

To be successful, learners should demonstrate robust knowledge and understanding of the unit in all tax areas. Learners cannot avoid any of the key topics and to ensure success, must be prepared to answer written and computational style questions in any of the tasks.

The Personal Tax assessment consists of 11 tasks:

Task	Maximum marks	Title for topics within task range
1	9	Benefits in Kind – provision of cars
2	10	Benefits in Kind – all excluding cars
3	10	Income from property
4	6	Investment income
5	12	Computation of total and taxable income
6	10	Computation of tax payable and payment of tax
7	10	Theory underpinning topic and penalties
8	7	Tax returns
9	12	Basics of capital gains tax
10	8	Taxation of shares
11	6	Capital gains tax exemptions, losses, reliefs and tax payable

QCF Level descriptor	**Summary**
	Achievement at Level 4 reflects the ability to identify and use relevant understanding, methods and skills to address problems that are well defined but complex and non-routine. It includes taking responsibility for overall courses of action as well as exercising autonomy and judgement within fairly broad parameters. It also reflects understanding of different perspectives or approaches within an area of study or work.
	Knowledge and understanding
	▪ Practical, theoretical or technical understanding to address problems that are well defined but complex and non-routine
	▪ Analyse, interpret and evaluate relevant information and ideas
	▪ Be aware of the nature and approximate scope of the area of study or work
	▪ Have an informed awareness of different perspectives or approaches within the area of study or work
	Application and action
	▪ Address problems that are complex and non-routine while normally fairly well defined
	▪ Identify, adapt and use appropriate methods and skills
	▪ Initiate and use appropriate investigation to inform actions
	▪ Review the effectiveness and appropriateness of methods, actions and results
	Autonomy and accountability
	▪ Take responsibility for courses of action, including where relevant, responsibility for the work of others
	▪ Exercise autonomy and judgement within broad but generally well-defined parameters

AAT UNIT GUIDE (AQ2013)

Personal Tax (PTAX)

Introduction

The Personal Tax unit covers the key taxes payable by individuals, namely income tax and capital gains tax. It is a Level 4 unit for which learners need no prior knowledge. However, this unit links into some of the requirements for the Business Tax unit and many students find studying both taxation units advantageous.

Purpose of the unit

The general purpose of this unit is to enable learners to understand the impact and significance of taxation on individuals. All sources of income for individuals, such as employment income, capital gains, income from land and property and investment income are covered. By studying these taxes, learners can appreciate the tax implications for their own personal situation, and that of clients.

Learning objectives

This unit will enable learners to:

- Demonstrate an understanding of legislation and procedures relating to personal tax

- Understand the current taxation principles of income from employment, investment income, property income and capital gains tax

- Calculate income from all sources and apply relevant allowances, deductions and reliefs to prepare accurate income tax computations

- Calculate the income tax liability of an individual

- Calculate the capital gains tax liability of an individual

- Prepare accurate computations and complete sections of relevant tax returns

Delivery guidance

Employment income

Employment income is a key area of this unit and will feature in multiple tasks within the assessment.

Learners can expect questions on:

- The differences between, and indicators of, employment and self-employment

- The basis of assessment for employment income

BPP
LEARNING MEDIA

- Income assessable from employment income
- Computation of various benefits in kind, including:
  - Provision of cars, including low emission cars, and fuel for private motoring
  - Beneficial loans
  - Living accommodation, including job related accommodation
  - Use of assets
  - Pool cars
  - Vans, including zero emission vans, and fuel for private motoring
  - Other taxable and non-taxable benefits:
    - Provision of meals and food vouchers
    - Employers contribution to occupational pension schemes
    - Parking facilities
    - Sporting and recreational facilities
    - Provision of childcare
    - Mobile telephones
    - Annual staff parties
    - Long service and suggestion scheme awards
    - Assets transferred to/ bought by employees
    - Goodwill gifts
    - Private medical and health screening
    - Job related living accommodation
    - Late night taxis
    - Household costs for employees working from home
    - Removals expenses and benefits
    - Re-training and training expenses and benefits
    - Employees working away or on international work
    - Scholarships
    - Entertaining expenses
    - Gifts to employees
    - Cycles and subsidised transport
- Recognition of allowable expenses and deductions, including:
  - Mileage allowances
  - Expenses payments and reimbursed expenses
  - Charitable giving through a payroll deduction scheme

It is also expected that learners will be able to explain employment income in terms of providing basic advice to taxpayers. For instance, being able to explain how job related accommodation operates is as relevant as being able to compute the taxable benefit in kind of accommodation. Also, learners may be expected to explain how a potential benefit in kind can be adjusted to make it tax free.

Learners will mainly be required to complete computational style questions for this topic area, but some written tasks can also be expected.

Excluded topics:

Calculation of car benefit where the emission figures are not given

PAYE system

National insurance contributions

Property income

Income from property is an important aspect of income tax, and learners must be able to show knowledge of such income from a variety of sources.

Learners can expect questions on:

- Furnished and unfurnished property
- Rent a room schemes
- Furnished holiday lettings

Computation of rental income, associated expenses and profit or loss arising, are important. Learners need to know about the wear and tear allowance. In addition, learners must be able to apply the rules for any losses arising from these sources of income.

Written and computational style questions can be expected that explore both the amounts taxable and allowable, and also the knowledge that underpins this source of income.

Excluded topics:

Leases

Savings income

Both taxable and non-taxable savings income is expected to be covered.

In particular, learners can expect questions on:

- Bank interest
- Building society interest
- Dividends
- Individual savings accounts (ISAs)

The computations of gross interest received, tax deducted at source, net interest received and how the income is taxed within the tax computation of an individual can all be expected. Learners need to demonstrate that they understand how tax credits on dividends operate within an individual's tax computation.

These questions will be mainly computational in nature, but understanding of the rules may also be assessed. This is particularly so for the topic of ISAs.

Excluded topics:

Junior ISAs

National Savings and investments

Child benefit

Payment of tax

Learners will need to be able to collate different types of income subject to income tax and apply the rules for different tax bands and rates. This includes all rates for all levels and types of income.

The impact of pension payments on taxation liabilities, both occupational and private, will need to be understood. Such knowledge could be assessed through both computational and written style questions. The impact on the basic rate band needs to be understood together with how taxpayers with income falling in all tax bands receive tax relief on their pension payments. Also, learners should be able to explain the differences between occupational and private pensions.

The impact of giving to charity also needs to be understood. Giving through employment and direct gift aid needs to be understood, including the differences in how tax relief is obtained. Extension of the basic rate band applies also here.

Personal allowances must be understood, including the age allowance.

An understanding of the payments on account system is crucial with learners expected to answer questions that involve both the computational aspects of this payment system, and to provide explanations to clients on how they are worked out.

Excluded topics:

Complexities of pension payments, such as annual allowances or lifetime allowances

Taxpayers under the age of 16

Married couples allowances

Blind persons allowance

Transferable personal allowances

Written advice to clients

This area underpins all the other specific taxation areas assessed within this unit. Learners can expect written questions on:

- What taxation documentation individuals need to maintain and for how long
- The responsibilities individuals have for disclosing full and accurate information to HMRC
- The duties and responsibilities tax practitioners have to clients and HMRC
- The sources of tax information for individuals
- How the various penalties and interest are applied by HMRC in relation to filing and payment processes for income tax and capital gains tax

This topic area will be assessed via a free text written response from the learner. The questions will usually be client focused so learners will be expected to address their answers in a manner appropriate to such an audience.

Excluded topics:

Complex computations such as daily interest.

Tax returns

There are three areas which are assessable:

- Employment income
- Property income
- Capital gains

These are expected to be completed with accuracy and completed in conjunction with the learner's own figures, if appropriate.

Capital gains tax

Learners must appreciate who and what is taxable under this heading. The impact that relationships between connected persons have on disposal of chargeable assets needs to be understood.

Computations can be expected on:

- Chargeable assets being disposed of
- Enhancement expenditure
- Part disposals
- Chattels
- Share disposals, including matching rules, bonus issues and rights issues
- Exempt assets, including principal private residence

Learners also need to be able to appropriately apply the annual exempt amount and understand how relief for losses work. Finally, learners must be able to compute the actual capital gains tax payable, based on the individual's income tax situation.

This topic will mainly be assessed via computational style questions, but learners must also be able to show understanding of the rules that underpin this topic.

Excluded topics:

Takeovers and reorganisations

Business reliefs such as rollover, gift and entrepreneurial relief

Small part disposals of land

Small part disposals rules as applicable to rights issues

TAXATION DATA

Taxation tables for personal tax – 2015/16

Note that 'TAXATION DATA 1' and 'TAXATION DATA 2' shown below will be available as pop up windows throughout your live assessment.

TAXATION DATA 1

Tax rates and bands

	%	£
Basic rate	20	first 31,785
Higher rate	40	to 150,000
Additional rate	45	over 150,000

Savings income is taxed at 0%, 20%, 40% and 45% (0% applies to a maximum of £5,000 of savings income only where non-savings income is below this limit). Dividends are taxed at 10%, 32.5% and 37.5%.

Personal allowances

	£
Personal allowance for individuals born after 5 April 1938	10,600
Age allowance for individuals born before 6 April 1938	10,660
Income limit for age allowance	27,700

TAXATION DATA 2

Car benefit percentage

Emission rating for petrol engines	%
0g/km to 50g/km	5
51g/km to 75g/km	9
76g/km to 94g/km	13
95g/km or more	14% + 1% for every extra 5g/km above 95g/km

Diesel engines – additional 3%

The figure for fuel is £22,100

Authorised mileage rates

First 10,000 miles   45p

Over 10,000 miles   25p

Van scale charge

	£
Charge	3,150
Private fuel provided	594
Zero emission van charge	630

HMRC official rate   3%

Capital gains tax

Annual exempt amount   £11,100

Tax rate   18%

Higher rate   28%

chapter 1:
THE TAX FRAMEWORK

chapter coverage 📖

In this chapter we see that individuals pay income tax on their taxable income, and capital gains tax on their taxable gains, and that the rules governing these taxes are laid down in both Acts of Parliament and a body of law known as case law.

Finally, we consider the responsibilities that tax practitioners have to clients and HM Revenue & Customs (HMRC), including client confidentiality.

The topics covered are:

✐ Tax position of individuals

✐ Relevant legislation and guidance from HMRC

✐ Responsibilities of tax practitioners

TAX POSITION OF INDIVIDUALS

Liability to tax

Individuals must pay **income tax on their taxable income**, and **capital gains tax on any taxable gains** arising on the disposal of chargeable assets. You will study income tax in the first part of this Text, and capital gains tax in the second part.

As a general rule, income is a receipt that is expected to recur (such as employment income), whereas a gain arises on a one-off disposal of a capital asset (eg the sale for a profit of a property held as an investment).

HM Revenue and Customs

Income tax and capital gains tax are administered by **HM REVENUE & CUSTOMS (HMRC)**.

Tax year

Individuals must prepare personal tax computations for tax years. A TAX YEAR, FISCAL YEAR, or YEAR OF ASSESSMENT, is the 12-month period that runs from 6 April in one year to 5 April in the next. For example, the **2015/16 tax year** runs from **6 April 2015 to 5 April 2016**.

In some cases, HMRC sends a taxpayer a tax return to be completed each tax year. However, most taxpayers have tax deducted from income before they receive it and this tax covers their tax liability so they are not sent a tax return by HMRC. We will look at tax returns in more detail when we consider the self-assessment system later in Chapter 6 of this Text.

RELEVANT LEGISLATION AND GUIDANCE FROM HMRC

Statute law

Most of the rules governing income tax and capital gains tax are laid down in STATUTE LAW, which consists of Acts of Parliament.

The existing Acts are amended each year (as a result of the Budget) in the annual Finance Act(s). In general election years there may be two or more Finance Acts, for example one before and one after the election. This Text includes the provisions of the **Finance Act 2015**. This Act will be assessed from January 2016.

Some tax Acts provide for the making of detailed regulations by STATUTORY INSTRUMENT (SI). An example is the regulations which set out how employers deduct tax from employees' earnings under the Pay As You Earn (PAYE) system.

An SI must be laid before Parliament and will usually become law automatically within a stated period unless any objections to it are raised.

Case law

Sometimes there may be a disagreement between HMRC and a taxpayer about how the tax legislation should be interpreted. In this situation either the taxpayer or HMRC may take the case to court. Cases about tax law are heard by the Tax Tribunal in the first instance.

Cases decided by the courts provide guidance on how legislation should be interpreted, and collectively form a second source of tax law known as CASE LAW.

You will not be expected to quote the names of decided cases in your assessment but you may need to know the principle decided in a case. Where relevant this will be noted within this Text.

HMRC guidance

To help taxpayers, HMRC publishes a wide range of guidance material on how it interprets tax law. These include:

(a) Statements of practice, setting out how HMRC intend to apply the law

(b) Extra-statutory concessions, setting out circumstances in which HMRC will not apply the strict letter of the law where it would be unfair. However these are being gradually codified or withdrawn as their legality has been challenged

(c) A wide range of explanatory leaflets

(d) Revenue & Customs Briefs. These give HMRC's view on specific points

(e) Internal Guidance, a series of manuals used by HMRC staff

(f) Working Together publications, for tax practitioners

Much of this information can be found on HMRC's website, **www.hmrc.gov.uk**.

However, none of HMRC's guidance material has the force of law. Although you may like to have a look at this website, you should find all you need for assessment purposes within this Text.

Task 1

Indicate with ticks which two of the following have the force of law.

	✓
Acts of Parliament	
HMRC Statements of practice	
Statutory Instruments	
Extra statutory concessions	

RESPONSIBILITIES OF TAX PRACTITIONERS

Responsibilities to clients and HMRC

Tax practitioners have a primary responsibility to act in the best interests of their clients. However, they also have a responsibility to deal with HMRC staff in a manner that is open and constructive and consistent with the law.

AAT Guidelines on Professional Ethics

The AAT publish *Guidelines on Professional Ethics,* which set out a code of fundamental ethical principles and supporting guidance. These relate to the responsibilities that tax practitioners have to clients and to HMRC.

There are five fundamental principles which AAT members must follow:

(a) **Integrity:** a member shall be straightforward and honest in all professional and business relationships

(b) **Objectivity:** a member shall not allow bias, conflict of interest or undue influence of others to override professional or business judgements

(c) **Professional competence and due care:** a member has a continuing duty to maintain professional knowledge and skill at the level required to ensure that a client or employer receives competent professional service based on current developments in practice, legislation and techniques. A member shall act diligently and in accordance with applicable technical and professional standards when providing professional services

(d) **Confidentiality:** see further below

(e) **Professional behaviour:** a member shall comply with relevant laws and regulations and avoid conduct that brings the profession into disrepute

Confidentiality

The *Guidelines* state that an AAT member must, in accordance with the law, **respect the confidentiality of information acquired as a result of professional and business relationships**, and **not disclose any such information** to third parties without proper and specific authority **unless there is a legal or professional right or duty to disclose**. The *Guidelines* also state that confidential information acquired as a result of professional and business relationships must not be used for the personal advantage of the member or third parties.

HOW IT WORKS

You act for Sarah in relation to her tax affairs. You and Sarah have a mutual friend, Jeremy. Sarah knows that you act for Jeremy in relation to his tax affairs and Sarah asks you to tell her whether Jeremy has invested in an ISA as she is considering making a similar investment.

You must inform Sarah that, due to client confidentiality, you cannot discuss another client's affairs, even if they are friends. However, if Jeremy gives you specific authority to disclose information about his investments to Sarah, you may do so.

Task 2

Cornelius is an acquaintance of your client, Ruby, as they have similar jobs in similar sized companies. He knows that Ruby was made redundant recently. He is facing redundancy himself and would like to know how much redundancy money Ruby received so that he can compare this to the figure his company is offering him.

State how you should reply to his request for this information, clearly justifying your reply.

Disclosure of information to HMRC

There are circumstances where the law allows a breach of the duty of confidentiality. The main situation where this arises for a tax practitioner is the requirement to produce information to HMRC.

HMRC usually informally requests information and documents from taxpayers in connection with their tax affairs. If, however, a taxpayer does not co-operate fully, **HMRC can request information and documents from a third party, such as a tax practitioner, by issuing a written 'information notice'**. An information notice issued to a third party must be issued with the agreement of the taxpayer or the approval of the Tax Tribunal.

Tax practitioners cannot be asked to produce information connected with tax advice they give to a client. For example, a tax practitioner may have to produce the detailed calculations used in the preparation of the taxpayer's return, say to value an asset, but not their reasons for choosing that method of calculation.

Material error or omission in client's tax return

The *Guidelines* state that when a member learns of a material error or omission in a tax return of a prior tax year or of a failure to file a required tax return, **the member has a responsibility to advise the client of the error or omission and recommend that disclosure be made to HMRC**.

If the client, after having had a reasonable time to reflect, does not correct the error, the member should inform the client in writing that it is not possible for the member to act for them in connection with that return or other related information submitted to the authorities.

The *Guidelines* further state that a member in practice whose client refuses to make disclosure of an error or omission to HMRC, after having had notice of it and a reasonable time to reflect, is obliged to report the client's refusal and the facts surrounding it to the Money Laundering Reporting Officer (see below) within the firm, or to the appropriate authority (National Crime Agency (NCA) in the UK) if the member is a sole practitioner. The member must not disclose to the client or any one else that such a report has been made if the member knows or suspects that to do so would be likely to prejudice any investigation which might be conducted following the report.

We look at the penalties that may be imposed on a client who makes a material error or omission in his tax return when we consider the self-assessment system later in Chapter 6 of this Text.

Money laundering

MONEY LAUNDERING occurs when the proceeds of criminal activities (including tax evasion) are converted into assets that appear to have a non-criminal origin.

AAT members are bound by legislation to implement preventative measures and to report suspicions to the appropriate authority. Failure to follow these legislative requirements will often be a criminal offence, leading to a fine and/or imprisonment. Firms must have appropriate procedures in place to ensure that knowledge and suspicions of money laundering are reported to the firm's Money Laundering Reporting Officer. A sole practitioner should make a report directly to the appropriate authority such as NCA.

Assessment focus

The information included in this chapter will typically be tested in the following task:

Task 7 – Theory underpinning topic and penalties

Performance feedback

The assessor's recent comments relevant to this chapter can be summarised as follows:

Students in this task have either failed to adequately understand basic areas, or they are not reading the questions carefully enough.

Students are encouraged to read about the topic areas covered in this task to ensure that they appreciate how a tax practitioner communicates and interacts with others.

CHAPTER OVERVIEW

- Individuals may have to pay income tax and/or capital gains tax

- HMRC is responsible for the administration of tax

- The tax year runs from 6 April in one year to the following 5 April

- Some of the rules governing tax are laid down in statute law, while some are laid down in case law

- HMRC provides guidance about how tax law works, for example in Statements of Practice, Extra Statutory Concessions and Revenue & Customs Briefs

- Tax practitioners have responsibilities to their clients and to HMRC

- The ethical *Guideline* of confidentiality means that a client's tax affairs should never be discussed with third parties without the client's permission

- Tax practitioners may be required to produce information to HMRC

- A tax practitioner must cease to act for a client who refuses to disclose an error or omission to HMRC, and must make a money laundering report

- Money laundering occurs when the proceeds of criminal activities are converted into assets which appear to have a non-criminal origin

Keywords

HM Revenue & Customs (HMRC) – responsible for the administration of tax

The Tax Year, **Fiscal Year** or **Year of Assessment** – the 12-month period that runs from 6 April in one year to 5 April in the next year. Thus the tax year 2015/16 runs from 6 April 2015 to 5 April 2016

Statute law – legislation contained in Acts of Parliament

Statutory instrument – sets out detailed regulations relating to tax as authorised in a tax Act

Case law – decisions of the courts about the interpretation of tax statutes and is also a source of tax law

Money laundering – proceeds of criminal activities converted into assets which appear to have a non-criminal origin

TEST YOUR LEARNING

Test 1

All taxpayers are sent a tax return each year by HM Revenue and Customs.

TICK ONE BOX.

	✓
True	
False	

Test 2

When is a tax practitioner not bound by the ethical *Guidelines* of client confidentiality?

TICK ONE BOX.

	✓
When in a social environment	
When discussing client affairs with third parties with the client's proper and specific authority	
When reading documents relating to a client's affairs in public places	
When preparing tax returns	

Test 3

Who should a sole practitioner make a report to if he suspects a client of money laundering?

TICK ONE BOX.

	✓
HMRC	
Nearest police station	
National Crime Agency	
Tax Tribunal	

Test 4

The tax administration within the UK is undertaken by:

TICK ONE BOX.

	✓
The Chancellor of the Exchequer	
Companies House	
HM Revenue & Customs	
Members of Parliament	

chapter 2:
TAXABLE INCOME

chapter coverage 📖

In this chapter we look at the income tax computation. There are three types of income that go into the income tax computation: non-savings, savings and dividend income. We also consider what types of income are exempt from income tax.

We see how to compute an individual's taxable income, including how to deduct a personal allowance or age allowance, which is an amount of income that is not taxable. This enables us to compute an individual's taxable income for a tax year.

The topics covered are:

✍ Non-savings, savings and dividend income

✍ Exempt income

✍ Computation of taxable income

NON-SAVINGS, SAVINGS AND DIVIDEND INCOME

Income tax computation

An INCOME TAX COMPUTATION is used to calculate an individual's income tax liability for a tax year. The income tax computation consists of the calculation of an individual's TAXABLE INCOME and the calculation of the individual's income tax liability by applying the relevant tax rates to the taxable income.

Different rates of tax apply to the three types of income in the income tax computation:

(1) Non-savings income
(2) Savings income
(3) Dividend income

Savings income and dividend income (along with property income, which is covered in Chapter 5) is also collectively known as 'investment income'.

The individual's tax liability is the amount of income tax that the individual should pay for the tax year. The actual amount of tax already paid by the individual during the tax year is then deducted from the income tax liability to give the income tax payable to HMRC or income tax repayable by HMRC to the individual.

It is therefore important to ensure that all income which is not exempt from income tax is included in the income tax computation gross, before any tax has been deducted at source.

Non-savings income

NON-SAVINGS INCOME is all income other than interest and dividends. The two main sources of non-savings income in the Personal Tax assessment are employment income and property income which we will cover in detail in later chapters of this Text. Other types of non-savings income include:

(a) Trading income: where an individual carries on a business as a sole trader or partner (dealt with in detail in Business Tax)

(b) Pension income

Savings income

SAVINGS INCOME is interest income. Interest can either be received **gross** or **net**.

If interest is received gross then no tax is deducted at source whereas if interest is received net, for example from a bank or building society, then 20% tax is deducted at source.

If an individual receives £80 of bank or building society interest, this is the NET amount and it must be grossed up by adding back the tax deducted at source. This is done by multiplying the net interest received by 100/80 to give £100 GROSS interest. It is this gross interest of £100 which appears in the income tax computation.

£100 is the gross interest that the individual has earned during the tax year but the bank or building society has already deducted 20% of this interest, being £20, at source and paid it over to HMRC on the individual's behalf. Therefore only £80 of net interest (ie 80% of the gross amount) is physically received.

The bank or building society always assumes that the individual is a basic rate taxpayer which is why tax at 20% is deducted at source. In fact, interest income can be taxed at 0%, 20%, 40% or 45% in the income tax computation depending on the amount of taxable income an individual has. We will look at this in more detail in Chapter 3.

In the assessment you may either be given the net or the gross amount of interest: read the question carefully. If you are given the net amount you should gross-up the figure by multiplying it by 100/80 as shown above. However, if you are given the gross amount, include the figure you are given in the income tax computation.

Most forms of interest are received net of tax such as bank or building society interest on current or savings accounts (also sometimes referred to as investment accounts), interest on fixed rate savings bonds or interest on loan stock issued by UK companies to individuals.

A savings bond is similar to a savings account except that it runs for a set period of time during which you may not be able to withdraw your money. In return, a savings bond tends to pay a higher rate of interest than a normal savings account.

Loan stock issued by UK companies is simply another method a company may use to borrow money from other companies or individuals instead of from a bank. The money is borrowed for a fixed term and there is a fixed interest rate paid.

An example of interest which is received gross (with no tax deducted at source) is interest on government securities (these are also called 'gilts') such as Exchequer Stock and Treasury Stock.

Task 1

Jesse receives building society account interest of £160, and interest of £60 from Treasury stock.

The total amount of interest to be included in his income tax computation is:

£ | 260

Dividend income

DIVIDEND INCOME is dividends received from a company in which the taxpayer owns shares. **Dividends are always received net of a deemed 10% tax credit** and therefore must be grossed up by multiplying the NET dividend received by 100/90 to give the GROSS dividend. It is this gross dividend which appears in the income tax computation.

This means a dividend received of £90 has a £10 tax credit, giving gross income of £100 (£90 × 100/90) to be included in the income tax computation.

It is important to realise that no tax has actually been deducted at source by the company paying the dividend, but the dividend received is **deemed** to be 90% of the gross amount. Therefore the deemed tax credit attached to dividends cannot be repaid to non-taxpayers but it can be offset against a taxpayer's tax liability. We see how to compute a taxpayer's tax liability in Chapter 3.

Task 2

Maria receives dividends of £900 and building society interest of £1,600.

The gross amount of dividends to be included in her income tax computation is:

£ | 1000

and the gross amount of interest to be included in her income tax computation is:

£ | 2000

EXEMPT INCOME

Some income is exempt from income tax. You must not include this income in the income tax computation.

In your assessment you should always state if income is exempt. If you do not, you may not be awarded the available mark.

Individual savings accounts (ISAs)

An individual savings account (ISA) is a special tax exempt way of saving. For tax year 2015/16, individuals can invest up to **£15,240** in an ISA.

The investment can be wholly in cash or wholly in stock market investments, units in unit trusts, fixed interest investments and life insurance policies, or a mixture of cash and other investments, subject to the overall limit above.

Dividends and interest received from investments in an ISA are exempt from income tax, whether paid out to the investor or retained and reinvested within the ISA. Any capital growth in the value of the ISA will also be free of capital gains tax (see later in this Text).

To open an ISA, an individual must be aged 18 or over, unless they open a 'Cash' ISA which holds cash only and is effectively a tax free savings account, in which case they only need to be aged 16 or over.

Individuals may open one ISA each tax year. It is possible to transfer ISAs between providers, and also to transfer a previous year's ISA investment in stocks and shares into a cash ISA.

Task 3

Denis receives the following (cash amounts):

Dividends from shares held within a ISA   ~~exempt~~   £360   36~~0~~ × 10~~0~~ ~~= 40~~
Interest on Treasury Stock   £180   ~~180 × 100 = 0~~ ~~= 40~~
Interest from NatWest Bank deposit account   £80   ~~20~~   ~~= 100~~

The total amount taxable on Denis is:

	✓
£280	✓
£500	✗
£100	
£680	

Other exempt income

Other exempt income includes:

(a) Damages for personal injury or death

(b) Scholarships and educational grants (exempt as income of the student – if paid by a parent's employer, a scholarship may be taxable income of the parent)

(c) Prizes, lotto winnings, gambling winnings

(d) Premium Bond prizes

COMPUTATION OF TAXABLE INCOME

Computing net income

For each tax year an individual may receive various 'components' of income. All income must be brought together in an income tax computation and is called TOTAL INCOME.

Certain expenses incurred by individuals called 'deductible payments' and relief for certain losses are then deducted from total income to give NET INCOME. Knowledge of these deductible payments is outside of the Personal Tax assessment. In your assessment either the term 'Total income' or 'Net income' may be used interchangeably. As mentioned earlier in the chapter, income in the income tax computation must be split into three types:

(1) Non-savings income
(2) Savings income
(3) Dividend income

HOW IT WORKS

In 2015/16, Margaret earns a salary of £30,000, receives gross interest of £1,000 and gross dividends of £1,000.

Her net income computation is:

	Non-savings income £	Savings income £	Dividend income £	Total £
Employment income	30,000			
Interest		1,000		
Dividends			1,000	
Net income	30,000	1,000	1,000	32,000

Task 4

Tracey has the following income in 2015/16.

	£
Business income	44,000
Building society interest (gross)	2,000
Dividends (gross)	1,000
Lotto winnings	10

Using the preceding proforma as a guide, show Tracey's net income split into non-savings, savings and dividend income.

Personal allowance

All persons (including children) **who were born after 5 April 1938 are entitled to a personal allowance (PA)** for 2015/16 **of £10,600**, but this is reduced for individuals whose net income exceeds £100,000.

Assessment focus

Within the assessment, if the age or date of birth of the taxpayer is not given, you should assume the person is born after 5 April 1938 and therefore entitled to the basic personal allowance of £10,600 (subject to reduction if income exceeds £100,000 as shown below).

The personal allowance (or the age allowance – see below) is deducted from net income to arrive at TAXABLE INCOME. The allowance is deducted first from non-savings income, then from savings income, and any remaining allowance from dividend income.

HOW IT WORKS

In 2015/16, Joe, who was born in June 1989, has trade profits of £3,000, receives bank interest of £14,000 and dividends of £450. Joe's taxable income for 2015/16 is:

	Non-savings income £	Savings income £	Dividend income £	Total £
Trade profits	3,000			
Bank interest (× 100/80)		17,500		
Dividends (× 100/90)			500	
Net income	3,000	17,500	500	21,000
Less personal allowance	(3,000)	(7,600)	–	(10,600)
Taxable income	–	9,900	500	10,400

Task 5

John, who was born in 1969, has trade profits of £11,160 in 2015/16. He also received building society interest of £2,000, premium bond prizes of £250 and dividends of £4,500.

Show John's taxable income for 2015/16.

Net income over £100,000

If an individual's net income exceeds £100,000, the personal allowance is reduced by £1 for each £2 by which net income exceeds £100,000.

HOW IT WORKS

In 2015/16, Kelvin has gross employment income of £98,000, receives building society interest of £1,200, damages of £1,500 for personal injury following a fall and dividends of £4,500. Kelvin's taxable income for 2015/16 is:

	Non-savings income £	Savings income £	Dividend income £	Total £
Employment income	98,000			
Building society interest		1,500		
(× 100/80)				
Dividends (× 100/90)			5,000	
Net income	98,000	1,500	5,000	104,500
Less personal allowance (W)	(8,350)	–	–	(8,350)
Taxable income	89,650	1,500	5,000	96,150

Damages for personal injury are exempt from income tax.

Working

	£
Net income	104,500
Less income limit	(100,000)
Excess	4,500
Personal allowance	10,600
Less half excess (4,500/2)	(2,250)
Adjusted personal allowance	8,350

Task 6

In 2015/16, Zelda has employment income of £97,500, receives bank interest of £4,000 and dividends of £2,250.

The personal allowance that Zelda is entitled to in 2015/16 is:

£ _____

There is also a special rule relating to the calculation of the personal allowance where, during the tax year, the taxpayer has made:

(a)   A Gift Aid donation, and/or
(b)   A contribution to a **personal** pension scheme

The rule is that for the purposes of comparing *net income* with the income limit of £100,000, the net income is reduced by the gross amount of the Gift Aid donations and personal pension contributions. This amount is known as the *adjusted net income*.

Note that this rule **only** applies when calculating the personal allowance, we will look at how tax relief is given for these payments in more detail in Chapter 3. You may want to review this rule after studying that chapter.

HOW IT WORKS

Millie has net income of £108,500 in 2015/16. Millie also makes a personal pension contribution of £2,000 (gross) in 2015/16.

Millie's personal allowance is calculated as follows:

	£
	£
Net income	108,500
Less gross personal pension contribution	(2,000)
Adjusted net income	106,500
Less income limit	(100,000)
Excess	6,500
Personal allowance	10,600
Less half excess (6,500/2)	(3,250)
Adjusted personal allowance	7,350

Task 7

Ernest has net income in 2015/16 of £109,000 and he makes a Gift Aid donation of £500 (gross) in January 2016.

Ernest is entitled to a personal allowance in 2015/16 of:

£ _____

Age allowance

A person who was born before 6 April 1938 receives a higher age allowance of £10,660 instead of the personal allowance of £10,600.

If the individual's net income exceeds £27,700, the age allowance is reduced by £1 for each £2 by which net income exceeds £27,700. The age allowance cannot however be reduced below £10,600 (unless net income is above £100,000, then the restriction above also applies).

The special rule which allows net income to be reduced by the gross amount of Gift Aid donations and personal pension contributions also applies in the calculation of the age allowance.

HOW IT WORKS

In 2015/16, Keith, who was born on 6 June 1930, has gross pension income of £21,800, receives building society interest of £1,600, damages of £1,500 for personal injury following a fall and dividends of £3,600. Keith's taxable income for 2015/16 is:

	Non-savings income £	Savings income £	Dividend income £	Total £
Pension income	21,800			
Building society interest (× 100/80)		2,000		
Dividends (× 100/90)			4,000	
Net income	21,800	2,000	4,000	27,800
Less age allowance (W)	(10,610)	–	–	(10,610)
Taxable income	11,190	2,000	4,000	17,190

Damages for personal injury are exempt from income tax.

Working

	£
Net income	27,800
Less income limit	(27,700)
Excess	100
Age allowance	10,660
Less half excess (100/2)	(50)
Adjusted age allowance	10,610

Task 8

In 2015/16, Zebedee, who was born in March 1935, has pension income of £21,000, receives bank interest of £2,000 and dividends of £4,500.

The age allowance that Zebedee is entitled to in 2015/16 is:

£

Assessment focus

In the live assessment you will be provided with 'Taxation Data' that can be accessed through pop-up windows. The content of these taxation data tables has been reproduced at the front of this Text.

The personal allowance, age allowances and income limit for the age allowance covered in this chapter are included within the taxation data pop-up. Make sure you familiarise yourself with the content and practise referring to it as you work through this Text.

This chapter covers the calculation of the gross income which should be included in the income tax computation and the deduction of the personal allowance or age allowance. Chapter 3 will then focus on how we calculate the tax payable on this taxable income.

In the Personal Tax assessment tasks may just focus on the calculation of the gross income or they may also require the calculation of the tax payable on that income.

The information included in this chapter will typically be tested in the following tasks:

Task 4 – Investment income

Task 5 – Computation of total and taxable income

Performance feedback

The assessor's recent comments relevant to this chapter can be summarised as follows:

Overall, the success rate for this task is very high at 84%, hence showing that learners fully appreciate the detail behind this topic area.

The main recurring errors are grossing up using the wrong percentage – 10% being applied to building society interest or 20% being applied to dividends – and confusion over the order in which such income is taxed. An example of this can be seen in the sample assessment for PTAX FA13 where there are three sources of investment income and learners need to show that they understand several things:

(1) Interest from ISA's is tax free

(2) Interest from building societies is taxed at source at 20%

(3) Dividends carry a tax credit of 10%

(4) Interest from building societies is taxed within a tax computation before dividends. This is a crucial point especially when different rates of tax need to be applied, as in this question.

It is the latter point that appears to cause learners the most difficultly and hence needs to be studied in great depth.

Further detail of the assessor's comments re these tasks is provided within the assessment focus at the end of Chapter 3.

A note about rounding

The AAT will allow you to show tax calculations either to the nearest pound or to the nearest pence – both answers will be marked correctly. In this Text we round tax calculations to the nearest pound.

When rounding is needed for an answer to an example or task, this Text has used the mathematical rounding rule of 0.5 and above being rounded up and anything below 0.5 being rounded down.

The AAT have told us that the computer will compensate for rounding differences and will accept a variety of answer formats (eg nil, NIL, Nil, 0, Zero ZERO).

However, always read the instructions provided by the AAT at the start of your assessment very carefully, as guidance will be given on how to input your answers. If any specific rounding rules are to be used they will be included within the guidance.

CHAPTER OVERVIEW

- There are three types of income in the income tax computation: non-savings, savings and dividend

- Non-savings income includes employment income, property income, trading (or business) income and pension income

- Savings income is interest received

- If an individual receives interest net of 20% tax it must be grossed up by multiplying by 100/80

- Dividends are received net of a deemed 10% tax credit. Dividends are grossed up by multiplying by 100/90

- Exempt income includes income from individual savings accounts (ISAs) and gambling winnings

- Tax computations must be prepared for a tax year

- All the components of an individual's income are added together to arrive at 'net income'

- Net income less the personal allowance or age allowance gives 'taxable income'

- The personal allowance is deducted first from non-savings income, then from savings income and finally from dividend income. It is reduced by £1 for every £2 that the individual's net income exceeds the income limit of £100,000

- The age allowance is given to individuals born before 6 April 1938. It is reduced by £1 for every £2 that the individual's net income exceeds the income limit of £27,700, but cannot be less than the personal allowance

- The net income figure for comparison to the income limit for the personal allowance and the age allowance is reduced by gross Gift Aid donations and personal pension contributions

Keywords

Non-savings income – income other than interest and dividends

Savings income – interest received, for example from a bank or building society

Dividend income – dividends received from a company

Total income – the total of an individual's income from all sources

Net income – an individual's total income less deductible payments and loss relief

Taxable income – an individual's net income minus the personal allowance or the age allowance

TEST YOUR LEARNING

Test 1

Classify the following types of income by ticking the correct box:

	Non-savings income	Savings income	Dividend income
Employment income	☐	☐	☐
Dividends	☐	☐	☐
Property income	☐	☐	☐
Bank interest	☐	☐	☐
Pension income	☐	☐	☐
Interest on government stock	☐	☐	☐

Test 2

Complete the table below to show the amount of income that would be included in a tax return for 2015/16. If your answer is zero please put a '0'.

	Amount received £	Amount in tax return £
Building society interest	240	
Interest on an individual savings account	40	
Dividends	144	
Interest from government gilts	350	

Test 3

In 2015/16 Joe has employment income of £30,000, receives dividends of £270 and premium bond winnings of £500.

Use the table below to show his taxable income for 2015/16.

Test 4

Pratish receives property income of £3,000 and building society interest of £7,200 in 2015/16.

Use the table below to show his taxable income for 2015/16.

Test 5

Jesse has employment income of £112,200 in 2015/16. He also received building society interest of £4,000, a prize of £50 in an internet competition and dividends of £3,600.

Use the table below to show Jesse's taxable income for 2015/16.

Test 6

Zoreen was born on 10 May 1937. In 2015/16, she receives pension income of £20,380, bank interest of £4,000 and dividends of £5,400.

The age allowance available to Zoreen for 2015/16 is:

£ [ ]

Test 7

The tax credit attached to a dividend can be offset against a taxpayer's tax liability, and if it exceeds the liability the taxpayer can receive a repayment.

TICK ONE BOX.

	✓
True	
False	

2: Taxable income

chapter 3:
CALCULATION OF INCOME TAX

chapter coverage 📖

In the last chapter you saw how to compute an individual's taxable income. In this chapter you will see how to compute the income tax liability and the income tax payable on this income.

The topics covered are:

✍ Calculating the income tax liability

✍ Calculating the income tax payable

CALCULATING THE INCOME TAX LIABILITY

Income tax bands

In Chapter 2 we saw how to compute taxable income. We now see how to compute the **income tax liability** on this taxable income.

First, the taxable income needs to be divided into three bands:

(1)   The first £31,785 of taxable income is in the BASIC RATE BAND

(2)   The next £118,215 of taxable income is in the HIGHER RATE BAND (from the higher rate threshold of £31,785 up to the ADDITIONAL RATE THRESHOLD of £150,000)

(3)   The remaining income is income in the ADDITIONAL RATE BAND which is income over the ADDITIONAL RATE THRESHOLD of £150,000

The rate of tax applied to the income in each band depends on whether the income is non-savings income, savings income or dividend income.

There is only one set of income tax bands used for all three types of income. These bands must be allocated to taxable income in the following order:

(1)   Non-savings income
(2)   Savings income
(3)   Dividend income

There is a special rule where the taxpayer has little or no non-savings income but has savings income. We deal with this later in this chapter.

Computing the tax liability

You need to calculate the income tax liability on taxable income as follows:

(1)   Deal with non-savings income first:

- Non-savings income in the basic rate band is taxed at **20%**
- Non-savings income in the higher rate band is taxed at **40%**
- Non-savings income above the additional rate threshold is taxed at **45%**

(2)   Second, deal with savings income:

If any of the basic rate band remains after taxing non-savings income it can be used here.

- Savings income that falls within the basic rate band is taxed at **20%**
- Savings income that falls within the higher rate band is taxed at **40%**
- Once savings income is above the additional rate threshold, it is taxed at **45%**

(3) **Third, compute tax on dividend income:**

- If dividend income falls within the basic rate band, it is taxed at **10%** (not 20%)

- Dividend income that falls within the higher rate band is taxed at 32.5%

- If, however, the dividend income exceeds the additional rate threshold, it is taxed at 37.5%

(4) **Total the tax = tax liability**

Add the above amounts of tax together. The resulting figure is the income tax liability.

HOW IT WORKS

Sasha has taxable income of £41,120. Of this, £29,920 is non-savings income, £6,000 is savings income and £5,200 is dividend income.

The non-savings income of £29,920 is all in the basic rate band. £1,865 of the interest uses the remaining basic rate band. £4,135 of interest and all the dividends are above the higher rate threshold of £31,785.

The income tax liability is:

		Income tax £
(1)	**Non-savings income**	
	£29,920 × 20%	5,984
(2)	**Savings income**	
	£1,865 × 20%	373
	£31,785	
	£4,135 × 40%	1,654
(3)	**Dividend income**	
	£5,200 × 32.5%	1,690
	£41,120	
(4)	**Income tax liability**	9,701

Task 1

Talet has taxable income of £60,000 for 2015/16. £25,000 of her taxable income is non-savings income. The remaining £35,000 is savings income.

Her income tax liability is:

£ [ ]

HOW IT WORKS

Nathan has taxable income of £185,000. Of this, £120,000 is non-savings income, £40,000 is savings income and £25,000 is dividend income.

The non-savings income of £120,000 uses all the basic rate band of £31,785 and £88,215 of the higher rate band. £30,000 of the interest uses the remaining higher rate band. £10,000 of interest and all the dividends are above the additional rate threshold of £150,000.

The income tax liability is:

		Income tax £
(1)	**Non-savings income**	
	£31,785 × 20%	6,357
	£88,215 × 40%	35,286
(2)	**Savings income**	
	£30,000 × 40%	12,000
	£150,000	
	£10,000 × 45%	4,500
(3)	**Dividend income**	
	£25,000 × 37.5%	9,375
	£185,000	
(4)	**Income tax liability**	67,518

Task 2

Stacey has total taxable income of £175,000 for 2015/16. Of this £110,000 is non-savings income and £65,000 is dividend income.

Stacey's income tax liability is:

£ [   ]

Savings income starting rate

There is a special rule where the taxpayer has little or no non-savings income but has savings income.

In this case, **there is a starting rate of 0% for the first £5,000 of savings income**. This is called the SAVINGS INCOME STARTING RATE BAND and is included within the basic rate band of £31,785, NOT in addition to it.

The savings income starting rate only applies where savings income falls within the savings income starting rate band. Remember that income tax is charged first on non-savings income. In most cases, an individual's non-savings income will exceed the savings income starting rate band, which will mean that savings income will fall in the basic rate band (20%) or higher rate band (40%) or above the additional rate threshold (45%).

However, if an individual's non-savings income does not use up the savings income starting rate band of £5,000, then savings income will be taxable at the 0% savings income starting rate within that band.

HOW IT WORKS

Tamara has taxable income of £10,000 in 2015/16. £2,000 is non-savings income and £8,000 is savings income. Her income tax liability is:

	Income tax £
Non-savings income	
£2,000 × 20%	400
Savings income	
£(5,000 − 2,000) = £3,000 × 0%	0
£(8,000 − 3,000) = £5,000 × 20%	1,000
Income tax liability	1,400

HOW IT WORKS

Thomas has taxable income of £35,000 in 2015/16. £1, ...on-savings income and £34,000 is savings income. His income tax liability is:

	Income tax £
Non-savings income	
£1,000 × 20%	200
Savings income	
£4,000 × 0%	0
£5,000	
£26,785 × 20%	5,357
£31,785	
£3,215 × 40%	1,286
£35,000	
Income tax liability	6,843

Task 3

In 2015/16, Joe earns a salary of £11,160 from a part-time job and receives bank interest of £8,000.

Joe's income tax liability for 2015/16 is:

£ [   ]

Extending the basic rate band

We have seen above that an individual normally has a basic rate band of £31,785 in 2015/16. There are two circumstances in which the basic rate band must be increased. These are when the individual pays:

(a) A **Gift Aid donation**, and/or
(b) A contribution to a **personal pension scheme**

A Gift Aid donation is a particular type of donation to charity on which tax relief is available.

Tax relief for personal pension contributions and Gift Aid donations

If an individual is employed and makes contributions into an employer's **occupational pension scheme**, the employee obtains tax relief by the employer deducting the employee's contribution from the employee's earnings before those earnings are taxed. In essence this means the employer administers the pension and **tax relief is automatically given** at the rate applicable to the individual.

For example if an individual had a salary of £100,000, and paid £10,000 into an occupational pension scheme, this would be deducted from the salary, leaving only £90,000 to pay tax on. This £10,000 would have been taxed at the higher rate of 40%, therefore the individual receives tax relief at 40% on the contribution. We will see this again when we cover Employment income in Chapter 4.

An individual who pays into a **personal pension scheme** will also be entitled to tax relief at his applicable rate of tax.

(a) **Basic rate tax relief is obtained by paying the contribution net of 20% tax**, thereby obtaining basic rate relief at the point of payment

(b) **Higher or additional rate relief is obtained by extending the basic rate band**

Both Gift Aid donations and contributions to personal pension schemes are paid net of 20% tax. For example, if an individual pays a pension contribution of £800, the gross amount of the donation is £800 × 100/80 = £1,000 (the individual contributes £800 into his scheme, and the government pays £200 into the scheme).

If the individual is a basic rate taxpayer, no further adjustments need to be made.

If the taxpayer is liable to tax at the higher rate, further relief is given. However, this must take account of the fact that basic rate relief has already been given. This is done by **extending the basic rate band by the gross amount of a Gift Aid donation and/or the gross amount of any personal pension contribution paid by the individual**. This means that taxable income equivalent to the gross payment will be taxed at the basic rate instead of the higher rate.

HOW IT WORKS

Gustav has taxable income (all non-savings) of £50,000 in 2015/16.

Assuming that Gustav does not make any Gift Aid donations nor personal pension contributions in 2015/16, his income tax liability will be:

	£
£31,785 × 20%	6,357
£18,215 × 40%	7,286
£50,000	13,643

Now think about the situation where Gustav makes a Gift Aid donation of £8,000 in 2015/16. The Gift Aid donation will have been paid net of 20% tax. This means that the gross amount of the payment is £8,000 × 100/80 = £10,000 and Gustav's basic rate band must be extended by £10,000. His income tax liability is calculated as follows:

	£
£31,785 × 20%	6,357
£10,000 (extended basic rate band) × 20%	2,000
£8,215 × 40%	3,286
£50,000	11,643

Extending the basic rate band means that £10,000 more income is taxed at the basic rate and therefore £10,000 less income is taxed at the higher rate. The difference between the tax liabilities without and with the Gift Aid donation is £10,000 × (40 − 20)% = £2,000. The total tax relief is:

	£
Basic rate relief given by net payment	2,000
Higher rate relief given by extending basic rate band	2,000
Total tax relief (which equates to 40% of the gross donation)	4,000

Task 4

In 2015/16 Hans has taxable income of £50,000. £24,000 of this income is non-savings income, the rest is savings income. Hans pays a personal pension contribution of £5,600 in 2015/16.

Hans' income tax liability for 2015/16 is:

[handwritten: 2400   26000]
[handwritten: 10,600]
[handwritten: 13,400   26000 - 39,400]

£ _____

[handwritten: 13400 × 20% = 2680]
[handwritten: 26000 × 20% = 5200]

If the taxpayer is liable to tax at the additional rate, extra relief is given. The higher rate band remains equal to £118,215. Extending the basic rate band therefore pushes the additional rate threshold up by the same amount so that taxable income equivalent to the gross payment is taxed at the basic rate instead of the additional rate.

HOW IT WORKS

Lara has taxable income (all non-savings) of £180,000 in 2015/16.

Assuming that Lara does not make any Gift Aid donations or personal pension contributions in 2015/16, her income tax liability will be:

	£
£31,785 × 20%	6,357
£118,215 × 40%	47,286
£30,000 × 45%	13,500
£180,000	67,143

Now think about the situation where Lara makes a personal pension contribution of £16,000 in 2015/16. The contribution will have been paid net of 20% tax. This means that the gross amount of the payment is £16,000 × 100/80 = £20,000 and Lara's basic rate band must be extended by £20,000.

Her income tax liability is calculated as follows:

	£
£31,785 × 20%	6,357
£20,000 (extended basic rate band) × 20%	4,000
£118,215 × 40%	47,286
£10,000 × 45%	4,500
£180,000	62,143

The difference between the tax liabilities without and with the Gift Aid donation is £20,000 × (45 – 20)% = £5,000. The total tax relief is:

	£
Basic rate relief given by net payment	4,000
Additional rate relief given by extending basic rate band	5,000
Total tax relief (which equates to 45% of the gross contribution)	9,000

CALCULATING THE INCOME TAX PAYABLE

We have seen above how to calculate the income tax liability on non-savings, savings and dividend income. Once this is done there are two final adjustments to be made in order to arrive at the tax payable, which is the balance of the liability still to be settled by the taxpayer.

(1) Deduct the tax credit on dividends from the tax liability. Although deductible, **this tax credit cannot be repaid** if it exceeds the income tax liability.

Task 5

Doris received dividend income of £22,500 in 2015/16. She has no other income.

The tax payable is:

£ [   ]

---

(2) Finally deduct any tax deducted at source on savings income, and any tax deducted under the PAYE system by an employer on employment income. We will see this in Chapter 4.

These amounts of tax suffered can be repaid to the extent that they exceed the income tax liability.

HOW IT WORKS

Samantha has the following income and outgoings for 2015/16.

	£
Gross salary (tax deducted by employer £3,000)	25,000
Dividend received (net)	2,000
Building society interest received (net)	16,400
Qualifying charitable donations paid under Gift Aid (gross amount)	300

Samantha's tax payable for 2015/16 is:

	Non-savings income £	Savings income £	Dividend income £	Total £
Employment income	25,000			
Building Society interest				
£16,400 × 100/80		20,500		
Dividends				
£2,000 × 100/90			2,222	
Net income	25,000	20,500	2,222	47,722
Less personal allowance	(10,600)			(10,600)
Taxable income	14,400	20,500	2,222	37,122

	£
Tax on non-savings income	
£14,400 × 20%	2,880
Tax on savings income	
£17,385 £(31,785 – 14,400) × 20%	3,477
£300 (extended basic rate band) × 20%	60
£2,815 × 40%	1,126
Tax on dividend income	
£2,222 × 32.5%	722
Income tax liability	8,265
Less tax credit on dividend income (£2,222 × 10%)	(222)
Less income tax suffered	

– on employment income (given)	3,000	
– on interest (£20,500 × 20%)	4,100	
		(7,100)
Income tax payable		943

Note. The basic rate band is extended by the gross amount of the Gift Aid donation.

Task 6

In 2015/16 Barry has rental income of £30,600, bank interest (net amount received) of £8,000, and dividends received of £10,800.

Compute Barry's income tax payable for 2015/16.

Task 7

Kate, who was born on 9 June 1936, has a gross salary of £16,115 (tax deducted by employer £1,100) and building society interest received of £4,000.

Calculate Kate's income tax payable for 2015/16.

Assessment focus

In the live assessment you will be provided with 'Taxation Data' that can be accessed through pop-up windows. The content of these taxation data tables has been reproduced at the front of this Text.

All the tax rates and bands covered in this chapter are included within the taxation data pop-up 1. Make sure you familiarise yourself with the content and practise referring to it as you work through this Text.

This chapter covers the calculation of both the income tax liability and the tax payable for a tax year. Make sure that you understand the difference between these two terms and calculate the right figure in the assessment.

The information included in this chapter will typically be tested in the following task:

Task 6 – Computation of tax payable and payment of tax

Performance feedback

The assessor's recent comments relevant to this chapter can be summarised as follows:

Whether income is received gross or net seems to cause the least issues, but computing actual tax payable on gross income based on an individual's tax situation is an issue.

Students do understand that the basic rate of tax that applies to dividends is 10%, but they are very poor at being able to use this information effectively. For example, if the tax credit is given, students struggle to convert that into a gross and net amount of dividend. Simple checking for logic would be useful as one student showed a tax credit of £50 as converting into £100 for gross and £80 for net.

Reading the question in detail is important as many students will show actual tax payable on a gross dividend at 10% for a higher rate taxpayer.

This task can cover income from all sources and the computation of tax on that income. It can cover all ages and all income brackets. Given that the questions can be quite challenging, it is very pleasing to see how well students perform.

The key to this task is taking time to digest the data before starting the answer. Note the age of the taxpayer first as many students fail to pick up on the age allowance. Once the taxable income has been established, make sure that the tax tables are used instead of relying on memory.

CHAPTER OVERVIEW

- Income is categorised into different types: non-savings, savings and dividend. Each type of income suffers different rates of tax depending on whether the income falls into the basic or higher rate bands or over the additional rate threshold

- Non-savings income is taxed first (at 20% then 40% then 45%) then savings income (at 0% then 20% then 40% then 45%) and finally dividend income (at 10% then 32.5% then 37.5%)

- The savings income starting rate of 0% applies to savings income within the savings income starting rate band

- Gift Aid donations and personal pension contributions are paid net of basic rate (20%) tax

- Extend the basic rate band by the gross amount of any Gift Aid donations and/or personal pension contributions paid by the taxpayer. This gives further tax relief to higher and additional rate taxpayers

- Deduct the tax credit on dividend income from the income tax liability. However, if it exceeds the income tax liability, the excess cannot be repaid

- Tax suffered on interest and tax deducted under the PAYE system is deducted in computing tax payable and can be repaid

Keywords

Basic rate band – the first £31,785 of income. The basic rate band may be extended by the gross amount of any Gift Aid donations and personal pension contributions paid by the taxpayer

Higher rate band – the next £118,215 of income. The upper limit to the higher rate band may be extended by the gross amount of any Gift Aid donations and personal pension contributions paid

Additional rate threshold – is the threshold over which income is taxed at the additional rate

Savings income starting rate band – applies if the taxpayer has non-savings income of less than this amount and also has savings income

TEST YOUR LEARNING

Test 1

At what rates is income tax charged on non-savings income?

TICK ONE BOX.

0%, 20%, 40% and 45%	✓
40% and 45%	
20% only	
20%, 40% and 45%	✓

Test 2

In 2015/16 Albert has a salary of £16,600, £2,000 (gross) of building society interest and £3,000 (gross) of dividends.

Albert's income tax liability is:

£ [   ]

$2000 \times \frac{100}{80} = 250$

$3000 \times \frac{100}{90} = 3333$

Test 3

In 2015/16 Carol has a salary of £5,000, and has received building society interest of £14,400 and a dividend of £19,800.

Carol's income tax liability is:

£ [   ]

Test 4

In 2015/16 Harry has a salary of £140,000, and has received building society interest of £16,000 and dividends of £27,000.

Harry's income tax liability is:

£ [   ]

Test 5

Explain how tax relief is given on Gift Aid donations.

BPP
LEARNING MEDIA

Test 6

Doreen, who was born in 1934, has the following sources of income in 2015/16.

	£
Gross pension income (tax deducted under PAYE £2,010)	17,000
Property income	3,500
Interest received from government stock	380
Dividends received	630
Premium bond prize	100

Calculate Doreen's income tax payable for the year.

Test 7

Sase has the following income and outgoings in 2015/16.

	£
Business profits	36,600
Building society interest received	4,000
Dividends received	3,600
Gift Aid donation paid	1,600

Compute Sase's income tax payable for the year.

Test 8

Vince is a higher rate taxpayer and makes a Gift Aid donation of £15,000 in 2015/16.

What is Vince's basic rate band in 2015/16?

TICK ONE BOX.

	✓
£46,785	
£31,785	
£43,785	
£50,535	

chapter 4:
EMPLOYMENT INCOME

chapter coverage 📖

In this chapter you start your studies of the calculation of employment income. We begin by considering how to decide whether an individual is employed or self-employed. We then learn about when earnings are received for tax purposes.

Next we see how to calculate the taxable value of employer-provided benefits, and consider what benefits are exempt from tax.

Then we look at some deductions that are allowable when computing taxable employment income.

We end the chapter by looking at the supplementary employment page that must accompany an individual's income tax return form.

The topics covered are:

✍ Employment and self-employment

✍ Taxation of employment income

✍ Taxable benefits

✍ Exempt benefits

✍ Allowable deductions

✍ Employment tax page

EMPLOYMENT AND SELF-EMPLOYMENT

When someone carries out work, it is important to be able to distinguish between employment (generating employment income) and self-employment (generating trading income).

- Employment is a contract **of** service
- Self-employment is a contract **for** services

It used to be thought that the deciding factor was the degree of control exercised by one party over the other about how the work should be done. The most that can be said now, however, is that control will always have to be considered, although it can no longer be regarded as the sole determining factor; other factors that may be of importance are such matters as:

(a) Whether the worker must be offered further work, and whether he must accept the work if offered (will indicate employment if this applies)

(b) Whether the person performing the services provides his own equipment (indicates self-employment)

(c) Whether he hires his own helpers (indicates self-employment)

(d) What degree of financial risk he takes (a high risk indicates self-employment)

(e) What degree of responsibility for investment and management he has (a high degree indicates self-employment)

(f) Whether and how far he has an opportunity of profiting from sound management in the performance of his task (indicates self-employment)

(g) Whether he can work when he chooses (indicates self-employment)

(h) Whether he is entitled to holiday and sickness pay (indicates employment)

(i) Whether he works solely for one organisation (indicates employment)

(j) The wording used in any agreement between the parties

In other words, the fundamental test to be applied is whether the person performing the services is performing them as a person in business on his own account. You may need to look at all of the above factors and form a view based on the balance of the evidence.

Task 1

Leon undertakes some work for LEO Plc. Tick whether the following factors would indicate that he has a contract of service (employment) or a contract for services (self-employment):

Factor	Contract of service	Contract for services
Leon must accept further work if offered	☐	☐
Leon hires his own helpers	☐	☐
Leon is entitled to paid holidays	☐	☐
Leon can profit from sound management	☐	☐

TAXATION OF EMPLOYMENT INCOME

Earnings from an office or employment are taxed as employment income.

In this assessment, earnings include:

(a) Salaries, wages, bonuses, commissions, fees and tips ('money earnings')

(b) Any benefits provided by the employer ('taxable benefits' or 'benefits in kind')

Certain allowable deductions can be made in the calculation of taxable earnings. We look at these later in this chapter.

When are earnings received?

Earnings generally are taxed in the tax year in which they are received.

Money earnings are treated as received at the earlier of:

(a) The time when payment is made; and
(b) The time when a person becomes entitled to payment of the earnings

HOW IT WORKS

Joy is employed by R plc. She is entitled to the payment of a bonus of £2,000 on 31 March 2016, although she does not receive it until 25 April 2016.

Joy will be taxed on the bonus in 2015/16 because she is entitled to payment on 31 March 2016.

Task 2

Rio is employed by BCD plc at an annual salary to 31 December 2015 of £20,000, and an annual salary to 31 December 2016 of £22,500. On 30 April 2016 he becomes entitled to and is paid a bonus of £5,000 relating to the company's profits for the year ended 31 December 2015.

Rio's earnings for 2015/16 are:

£ _____

If the employee is a director of a company, his earnings from the company are received on the earliest of:

(a) The time when payment is made

(b) The time when a person becomes entitled to payment of the earnings

(c) The time when the amount is credited in the company's accounting records

(d) The end of the company's period of account (if the amount is determined by then)

(e) The time the amount is determined (if after the end of the company's period of account)

HOW IT WORKS

Matt is a director of MN Ltd. On 25 March 2016, the company determines that it will pay Matt a bonus of £10,000 in relation to its period of account ending 31 March 2016. This is credited to Matt's director's account with the company on 10 April 2016 but he is not entitled to draw it until 30 April 2016. He actually draws out the payment from his account on 6 June 2016.

Matt is treated as receiving the bonus on 31 March 2016 (the end of the company's period of account) as the amount was determined by that time.

BPP
LEARNING MEDIA

Task 3

Rita is a director of RS Ltd. On 10 April 2016, the company determines that it will pay Rita a bonus of £15,000 in relation to its period of account ending 31 December 2015. This is credited to Rita's director's account with the company on 15 June 2016 but she is not entitled to draw it until 31 July 2016. She actually draws out the payment on 31 October 2017.

Rita receives the bonus on:

	✓
31 December 2015	
31 March 2016	
10 April 2016	
15 June 2016	
31 July 2017	
31 October 2017	

Taxable benefits are generally received when they are provided to the employee.

Deduction of income tax by employer

An employer is required to deduct income tax from employees' money earnings under the Pay As You Earn (PAYE) system. The employees therefore receive money earnings net of tax. The PAYE system also deals with taxable benefits. In most cases, this means that the employees have no further tax payable or repayable.

Details of the PAYE system are not in your syllabus.

In the assessment you will be given information about an employee's salary and then told the PAYE deducted from the salary – the salary given will be the gross salary (ie before PAYE has been deducted) unless you are told otherwise.

TAXABLE BENEFITS

Taxable benefits are set out in legislation called the Benefits Code. We will see below how certain benefits are taxed, however in the absence of any specific rule, the taxable benefit will be the **cost to the employer**.

Company cars

If a car is provided for **private use** by reason of a person's employment a taxable benefit arises. This is sometimes called a 'company car' benefit, although the rules apply whether the employer is a company or not. Private use includes home to work travel.

The benefit is normally a **percentage of the car's list price**.

The list price, for the purpose of calculating the benefit, is the sum of:

(a) The list price when new, including all standard accessories

(b) The cost of all optional extras fitted to the car before being made available to the employee (excluding mobile phones)

(c) The cost of all optional extras fitted later, costing at least £100

Note: Security enhancements will not count towards the list price.

The percentage (that the list price is multiplied by) is dependant on the car's CO_2 emissions rating (the number of grams of CO_2 emitted per kilometre travelled).

(a) For cars which emit CO_2 of up to 50 g/km the percentage is 5%

(b) For cars which emit CO_2 from 51 g/km up to 75 g/km the percentage is 9%

(c) For cars which emit CO_2 from 76 g/km up to 94 g/km the percentage is 13%

(d) For cars which emit CO_2 of 95 g/km or more the percentage is 14%, however this percentage increases by 1% for every additional whole 5 g/km of CO_2 emissions above 95 g/km, up to a maximum of 37%

The percentages are increased by 3% for diesel cars, again up to the maximum of 37%.

You will always be given a car's CO_2 emission rate in your assessment. If this is more than 95 g/km, your first step in calculating a car benefit should be to round this **down** to the nearest multiple of 5 g/km below the actual emissions. You then need to see by how many g/km the base figure of 95 g/km is exceeded. We show how this works in the following example.

HOW IT WORKS

Nigel is provided with a petrol engine car which had a list price of £22,000. The car has CO_2 emissions of 173 g/km.

Nigel's taxable car benefit for 2015/16 is calculated as follows:

First, round down 173 g/km to 170 g/km (the nearest figure divisible by 5).

Then calculate the amount by which the base figure is exceeded, in this case 75g/km (170 – 95).

Then divide this by 5, ie 75/5   = 15

Add this number to 14 to give a figure to be used as the percentage

ie the taxable percentage is 14% + 15%   = 29%

So the car benefit is £22,000 × 29%   = £6,380
                                                                                          ‾‾‾‾‾‾

If an employee makes a **capital contribution** towards the cost of a car, the contribution is **deducted from the list price** used for calculating the benefit, subject to a maximum deduction of £5,000.

If an employee makes a payment for the **private use of a car** such as running costs (as distinct from a capital contribution to the cost of the car), the payment is **deducted from the benefit figure** calculated.

The car benefit is pro-rated if the car is only provided for part of the year or if it is incapable of being used for 30 or more consecutive days.

HOW IT WORKS

Vicky starts her employment on 6 January 2016 and is immediately provided with a new petrol engine car with a list price of £25,000. The car was more expensive than her employer would have provided and she therefore made a capital contribution of £6,200. Vicky contributes £100 a month for being able to use the car privately. CO_2 emissions are 203 g/km. Vicky's car benefit for 2015/16 is:

	£
List price	25,000
Less capital contribution (maximum)	(5,000)
	20,000

£20,000 × 35% (W) = £7,000 (annual benefit)

	£
6 January 2016 to 5 April 2016 (3 months) = 3/12 × £7,000	1,750
Less contribution to running costs (£100 × 3)	(300)
Car benefit	1,450

Working

CO_2 emissions = 200 g/km (rounded down)

The amount by which the base figure is exceeded is 105 g/km (200 – 95).

105/5 = 21

Taxable percentage = 14% + 21% = 35%

Note petrol cars with CO_2 emissions of 210 g/km or more will use the maximum 37%.

The taxable car benefit covers all expenditure by the employer on repairs, servicing, insurance, road fund licence and cleaning of the car. No additional benefit arises in respect of these items. A taxable benefit does, however, arise in respect of a chauffeur provided for private mileage. This will be based on the cost of the chauffeur.

Task 4

On 6 July 2015 Sue was provided with a new petrol engine car by her employer. The list price of the car was £10,000. The car's CO_2 emissions are 189 g/km.

The taxable benefit on the provision of the car in 2015/16 is:

£ [   ]

Fuel provided for private use

If an employer pays for fuel used for private motoring in a company car, a fuel benefit arises.

The benefit is a percentage of a base figure.

(a)   The base figure for 2015/16 is £22,100

(b)   The percentage is the same percentage as is used to calculate the car benefit

No benefit arises where it can be shown that either all the fuel provided was used only for business travel or that the employee has reimbursed the employer for the whole of the expense of any fuel provided for his private use.

There is **no** reduction to the benefit if only part of the expense for private use fuel is reimbursed by the employee.

The fuel benefit is reduced if private fuel is not available for part of a tax year. However, if private fuel later becomes available again in the same tax year, there is no reduction made.

HOW IT WORKS

An employee was provided with a new petrol engine car costing £15,000 (the list price) on 6 June 2015. During 2015/16 the employer spent £900 on insurance, repairs and the vehicle licence. The firm paid for all petrol (£2,300) without reimbursement. The employee was required to pay the firm £25 per month for the private use of the car. The car has CO_2 emissions of 84 g/km.

The total taxable benefit for 2015/16 in respect of the car and fuel is calculated as follows:

	£
The car was available for ten months:	
List price £15,000 × 13%	1,950
£1,950 × 10/12	1,625
Less contribution (10 × £25)	(250)
	1,375
Fuel benefit £22,100 × 13% × 10/12	2,394
Total taxable benefit	3,769

If the contribution of £25 per month had been towards the petrol, the contribution would not be deducted, making the benefit assessable £250 greater. Conversely, if the cost of private petrol was fully reimbursed by the employee then there would have been no fuel benefit at all.

Task 5

Nissar had the use of a company car throughout 2015/16. The list price of the car was £30,000. The car had a diesel engine and CO_2 emissions of 164 g/km. The company provided fuel for both private and business motoring. Nissar made a contribution of £400 towards the cost of private fuel.

The total taxable benefit arising to Nissar in 2015/16 is:

£ [   ]

Pool cars

The private use of a pool car is an exempt benefit. A car is a pool car if all the following conditions are satisfied:

(a) It is used by more than one employee and is not ordinarily used by any one of them to the exclusion of the others

(b) Any private use is merely incidental to business use

(c) It is not normally kept overnight at or near the residence of an employee

BPP
LEARNING MEDIA

Vans provided for private use

Where a van is provided to an employee that is **available for private use**, there is an **annual scale charge of £3,150**.

There is not a taxable benefit if there is no private use allowed. Private use does not include home to work travel (compare to cars where home to work travel is private use).

If the van has **zero emissions**, then the benefit for 2015/16 is 20% of the normal van benefit (ie 20% × £3,150 = £630).

There is an **additional fuel benefit of £594 per annum if fuel is provided for private use**.

Assets made available for private use

In general, if an employee uses an employer-owned asset privately (other than cars and mobile phones), an **annual benefit arises equal to 20% of the market value of the asset when first used by the employee**.

If the asset is subsequently acquired by the employee, the benefit arising on the acquisition is usually the greater of:

(a)   The market value of the asset on acquisition

(b)   The market value of the asset when first provided to the employee less any amounts already assessed as a benefit

The greater of (a) or (b) is then reduced by any price paid by the employee to acquire the asset, to give the taxable benefit.

HOW IT WORKS

A suit costing £200 is bought by an employer for use by an employee on 6 April 2014. On 6 April 2015 the suit is purchased by the employee for £15, its market value then being £25.

The benefit taxable in 2014/15 will be 20% × £200 = £40

The benefit taxable in 2015/16 will be the greater of:

(a)   Market value at acquisition by employee = £25

(b)	£	£
Original market value	200	
Less assessed in respect of use 2014/15	(40)	
	160	
Therefore (b)		160
Less price paid by employee		(15)
Taxable benefit 2015/16		145

Task 6

Ahmed bought video equipment from his employer on 6 July 2015 for £1,000. The equipment was then worth £4,000. Ahmed had first used the equipment on 6 April 2014 when his employer had lent it to him for private use. Ahmed had sole use of the equipment from 6 April 2014 until he bought it on 6 July 2015. The market value of the equipment was £6,000 on 6 April 2014.

The taxable benefit for use arising in 2014/15 is:

£ [ ]

In 2015/16 is:

£ [ ]

The taxable benefit on Ahmed's acquisition in 2015/16 is:

£ [ ]

Beneficial loans

Employer loans to employees give rise to a benefit equal to:

(a) **Any amounts written-off**; and

(b) **The excess of the official rate of interest on the loan over any interest actually charged**

There are two methods of calculating the interest benefit. **The 'average' method applies automatically unless an election is made by the taxpayer or HMRC.** (HMRC normally only make the election where it appears that the 'average' method is being deliberately exploited.)

The first method averages the balance of the loan at the beginning and end of the tax year (or the dates on which the loan was made and discharged if it was not in existence throughout the tax year) and applies the official rate of interest to this average. If the loan was not in existence throughout the entire tax year, only the number of complete tax months (from the sixth of the month) for which it existed are taken into account.

The second method (the alternative or 'strict' method) is to compute interest at the official rate on a daily or monthly basis on the actual amount outstanding.

The official rate of interest will be 3% for the purpose of your assessment and will be provided in the 'Taxation Data' available throughout the assessment.

HOW IT WORKS

At 6 April 2015 a low interest loan of £30,000 was outstanding to a director, who repaid £20,000 on 6 January 2016. The remaining balance of £10,000 was outstanding at 5 April 2016. Interest paid during the year was £250.

The benefit under both methods for 2015/16, assuming that the official rate of interest was 3% throughout 2015/16, is calculated as follows:

Average method

	£
$3\% \times \dfrac{(30,000 + 10,000)}{2}$	600
Less interest paid	(250)
Taxable benefit	350

Alternative method

	£
£30,000 × 9/12 × 3%	675
(6 April 2015 – 6 January 2016)	
£10,000 × 3/12 × 3%	75
(6 January 20162015 – 5 April 2016)	
	750
Less interest paid	(250)
Taxable benefit	500

Therefore the taxable benefit will be £350.

No taxable benefit arises if the combined outstanding balance on all loans to the employee did not exceed £10,000 at any time in the tax year.

When the £10,000 threshold is exceeded, a benefit arises on interest on the whole loan, not just on the excess of the loan over £10,000.

When a loan is written-off and a benefit arises, there is no £10,000 threshold: writing-off a loan of £1 gives rise to a £1 benefit.

HOW IT WORKS

Annika has two loans from her employer throughout 2015/16:

(a) A season ticket loan of £2,300 at no interest
(b) A loan of £24,000 at 2% interest which Annika used to buy a holiday cottage

The official rate of interest is 3%.

As the total of the loans exceeds £10,000 a taxable benefit arises in respect of both loans.

The taxable benefit that arises in respect of the loans in 2015/16 is calculated as follows:

	£
£2,300 × 3%	69
£24,000 × (3% − 2%)	240
Taxable benefit	309

Task 7

On 6 April 2015 Anton's employer provided him with an interest-free loan of £11,200. He repaid £1,000 of this loan on 6 October 2015. The official rate of interest is 3%.

The taxable benefit arising in respect of the loan in 2015/16, assuming no elections are made, is:

£ [ ]

Task 8

An employer lends an employee £8,000 interest-free for six months. The official rate of interest is 3%. 65% of the loan is then repaid, and the balance is written-off.

The total taxable benefit is:

£ [ ]

Accommodation

If an **employer provides an employee with accommodation**, there is a **basic benefit** equal to the higher of:

(a) The 'annual value' of the property (given in the assessment); and

(b) Any rent actually paid for the property by the employer (if the property is rented rather than owned by the employer)

The benefit is reduced by any contribution the employee makes for the use of the property.

The benefit is exempt if the accommodation is job-related. The definition of job-related accommodation is covered later in this chapter.

HOW IT WORKS

Tony is provided with a company flat:

	£
Annual value	3,000
Rent paid by the company	3,380
Amount paid by Tony to the company for the use of the flat	520

Tony's taxable benefit is:

		£
Benefit: greater of:		
(a)	Annual value	3,000
(b)	Rent paid by the company	3,380
ie		3,380
Less reimbursed to the company		(520)
Net benefit		2,860

If the accommodation is owned by the employer and the cost of that accommodation exceeded £75,000, then an additional benefit arises. The amount of the **additional benefit** is equal to:

$$\text{ORI} \times (C - £75,000)$$

(a) ORI is the official rate of interest at the start of the tax year. This will be given to you in the assessment, and is 3% in 2015/16.

(b) C is the cost of providing the accommodation. This includes the cost of purchase and the cost of any improvements made before the start of the tax year under consideration.

If the **accommodation was acquired by the employer more than six years before it was first provided to the employee**, and its original cost plus improvements exceeded £75,000, the **'cost of providing' is increased to its market value when first provided** to that employee (plus the costs of subsequent improvements before the start of the tax year under consideration).

Where any contribution paid by the employee exceeds the annual value of the property, the excess may be deducted from the additional benefit.

HOW IT WORKS

Simon's employer provided him with a house throughout 2015/16. The company bought the house for £133,000 on 1 April 2011.

For 2015/16, the annual value of the house is £1,400. Simon pays £3,000 for the use of the house to his employer.

The total benefit arising in respect of the house for 2015/16, assuming the official rate of interest is 3% is:

Basic charge:

	£
Annual value	1,400
Less Simon's contribution	(1,400)
	Nil

Additional charge:

	£	£
Cost	133,000	
Less	(75,000)	
Excess		58,000
£58,000 × 3%		1,740
Less Simon's contribution (£3,000 – 1,400)		(1,600)
Total benefit 2015/16		140

Task 9

Throughout 2015/16 Marak lived in a house provided by his employer. The following information is relevant:

Annual value	£5,200
Cost of the house (bought by employer in 2014)	£600,000
Rent paid by Marak in 2015/16	£12,000
Official rate of interest throughout 2015/16	3%

The taxable value of the accommodation provided in 2015/16 is:

	✓
£3,750	
£8,950	
£20,950	
£15,750	

Expenses connected with living accommodation

The following living expenses ('ancillary services') incurred in connection with living accommodation give rise to a taxable benefit:

(a) Heating, lighting or cleaning the premises

(b) Repairing, maintaining or decorating the premises

(c) Providing furniture etc normal for domestic occupation (annual benefit taken as 20% of cost)

If the accommodation is job-related no accommodation benefit is chargeable (see below). In that case, the maximum chargeable benefit in respect of the above expenses is 10% of the employee's net earnings, ie salary plus all other taxable benefits less any allowable deductions.

Task 10

Mr Quinton has a gross salary in 2015/16 of £27,400. He is required to live in job-related accommodation.

The annual value of the house is £2,500.

In 2015/16 the company pays an electricity bill of £550, a gas bill of £400, a gardener's bill of £750 and redecoration costs of £1,800. Mr Quinton makes a monthly contribution of £50 for his accommodation.

Mr Quinton's taxable employment income for 2015/16 is:

£ [   ]

Vouchers

An employee is normally taxable on the cost to the employer of providing a voucher exchangeable for goods or services (non-cash voucher) or credit token (eg a credit card).

However, if the employee receives a voucher exchangeable for cash (cash voucher), he will be taxable on the amount for which the voucher can be exchanged.

There are some exemptions for specific vouchers. These are explained later in this chapter.

Approved mileage allowance payments

Where **employers pay mileage allowances to employees who use their own vehicles for business travel,** the employees are **taxed on any amounts received in excess** of the AUTHORISED MILEAGE RATES (AMR).

The authorised mileage rates for cars are:

(a)   45p a mile for the first 10,000 miles
(b)   25p a mile thereafter

There are separate mileage rates for motorcycles and bicycles. If you need any of these rates, they will be given to you in the assessment.

If the employer does not pay a mileage allowance to the employee, or if the allowance paid is less than the amount calculated using the authorised mileage rates, the **employee may deduct the shortfall as an allowable deduction/expense** when calculating taxable employment income.

HOW IT WORKS

Owen drives 14,000 business miles in 2015/16 using his own car.

You are required to calculate the taxable benefit/allowable deduction assuming:

(a)   He is reimbursed 45p a mile
(b)   He is reimbursed 25p a mile

	£
Statutory limit: 10,000 × 45p	4,500
4,000 × 25p	1,000
	5,500

(a)

	£
Amount received (14,000 × 45p)	6,300
Less statutory limit	(5,500)
Taxable benefit	800

(b)

	£
Amount received (14,000 × 25p)	3,500
Less statutory limit	(5,500)
Allowable deduction	(2,000)

Task 11

Yarrik used his car to travel 12,000 business miles in 2015/16. His employer paid him 42p per business mile travelled.

The taxable benefit/allowable deduction arising on Yarrik in respect of the amount paid to him by his employer is (both minus signs and brackets can be used to indicate negative numbers):

£ [   ]

Task 12

Megan uses her own car for business travel and her employer reimburses her 25p per mile. In 2015/16 Megan drove 12,000 business miles.

Megan's taxable benefit/allowable deduction is (both minus signs and brackets can be used to indicate negative numbers):

£ [   ]

EXEMPT BENEFITS

There is a fairly long list of benefits that are not taxable on employees, including:

(a) **Accommodation**

Living accommodation that constitutes JOB-RELATED ACCOMMODATION. Accommodation is job-related if:

(i) Residence in the accommodation is necessary for the proper performance of the employee's duties (eg a caretaker); or

(ii) Accommodation is provided for the better performance of the employee's duties and the employment is of a kind in which it is customary for accommodation to be provided (eg a vicar or policeman); or

(iii) The accommodation is provided as part of special security arrangements in force because of a special threat to the employee's security (eg the Prime Minister)

(b) **Subsistence**

  (i)   Meals in a staff canteen, if they are available to all employees on broadly similar terms, and as long as there is not a contractual entitlement to receive meals instead of cash. (These would be taxable)

  (ii) Personal incidental expenses of up to £5 per night for employees working away from home in the UK, or £10 per night if working abroad that would otherwise be taxable (eg laundry, newspapers, telephone calls home)

  However, where more than one night is spent away, the exemption works on an aggregate basis, eg for four nights working away from home in the UK the overall limit is £20. If the limit is exceeded, all the expenses are taxable, not just the excess.

(c) **Travel**

  (i)   Use of a pool car (see above)

  (ii) The provision of a parking space at or near the place of work

  (iii) Approved mileage allowance payments for cars, motor bikes and bicycles within the statutory limits (authorised mileage rates) (see above)

  (iv) The provision of works buses with a seating capacity of nine or more that are used mainly to bring employees to and from work

  (v)   The payment of general subsidies to public bus services used by employees to travel to work

  (vi) The provision of bicycles and cycling safety equipment made available for employees mainly to travel between home and work

  (vii) The cost of a taxi late at night when the employee is occasionally required to work late (ie after 9pm)

(d) **Removal expenses**: up to £8,000 of removal expenses borne by the employer where the employee has to move house on first taking up the employment or on a transfer within the organisation

(e) **Entertainment**: the provision of staff parties provided that the cost is no more than £150 per head per annum

(f) **Childcare**: the cost of running a workplace nursery or play scheme (without limit). Otherwise up to £55 a week (for basic rate taxpayers) is tax-free if the employer contracts with an approved child carer or provides childcare vouchers to pay an approved child carer. The weekly tax-free limits for higher and additional rate taxpayers are £28 and £25 respectively. The childcare must be available to all employees and the childcare must be registered or approved home childcare

(g) **Home-working**: a tax-free allowance of up to £4 per week is payable to employees to cover the additional household costs of working some or all of the time at home. No record keeping is required for the flat-rate allowance. For payments above that figure, evidence will be required that the payment is wholly in respect of additional household expenses incurred by the employee in carrying out their duties at home

(h) **Work-related training and related costs**: this includes the costs of training material and assets either made during training or incorporated into something so made

(i) **Payments by the employer to registered pension schemes**: to provide pension benefits for employees (see later in this chapter)

(j) **Miscellaneous**

   (i)   Non-cash long service awards – for service in excess of 20 years, £50 per year of service is tax-free

   (ii) Awards under a formally constituted staff suggestion scheme open to all employees on equal terms, for a suggestion outside the scope of the employee's normal duties. The award must either be not more than £25 or made after a decision is made to implement the suggestion. Awards over £25 must reflect the financial importance of the suggestion to the business. If an award exceeds £5,000, the excess over £5,000 is always taxable

   (iii) Workplace sports or recreational facilities provided by employers for use by their staff generally. This does not apply where the employer pays or reimburses an employee's subscription to a sports club, nor where the facilities are only available to limited groups of employees

   (iv) Air miles obtained in the course of business travel

   (v)   The private use of one mobile phone by the employee. If more than one mobile phone is provided to an employee for his private use or a phone is provided to a member of the employee's family, a taxable benefit arises based on the cost to the employer of provision of these phones

   (vi) Health-screening assessment or routine medical check ups provided for an employee, by the employer (maximum of one each per tax year). Provision of private medical insurance however, is taxable

   (vii) Officially recommended medical treatment, costing up to £500 per employee per year, to help the employee return to work after a period of absence due to ill-health or injury

(viii) Non cash gifts from third parties (sometimes referred to as goodwill gifts) up to £250 per tax year from the same donor. If the limit is exceeded, the full amount is taxable, not just the excess

(ix) Gifts which arise out of the employment are taxable unless they are given to the employee in a personal capacity (for example a wedding present)

ALLOWABLE DEDUCTIONS

The following expenditure can be deducted in the calculation of taxable earnings:

(a) Contributions by the employee to a **registered occupational pension scheme**

(b) Subscriptions to professional bodies, if relevant to the duties of employment

(c) Donations to charity under an **approved payroll deduction scheme**

(d) Qualifying travel expenses

(e) Other expenses incurred **wholly, exclusively and necessarily** in the performance of the duties of employment

These deductions are all made before the earnings are taxed, thereby giving tax relief at the rate applicable to the taxpayer.

We now look at these deductions in more detail.

Contributing to a pension

An individual may make pension provision in a number of ways.

If the individual is employed, he may join

(a) An **occupational pension scheme** run by his employer that is registered with HMRC and/or

(b) A **personal pension scheme** run by a financial institution such as an insurance company or a bank

If an individual is not employed, obviously he would only be able to join a personal pension scheme.

In order for a scheme to be approved or registered, it must comply with certain limits and regulations. **Tax relief is only available for contributions made to pension schemes which are registered with HMRC.**

There is a limit on the amount of contributions that an individual can make in a tax year. This limit applies to the total of all the pension arrangements that he makes, not *each* of them.

Each tax year an individual under the age of 75 may make tax-relievable pension contributions of up to the higher of:

(a) His earnings

(b) The basic amount (£3,600 in 2015/16)

Individuals with no earnings can, therefore, contribute £3,600 to a pension scheme each year.

Tax relief for the two schemes is quite different. Under the section 'Allowable deductions' above, this clearly refers to employee contributions to **occupational** pension scheme.

We saw how tax relief is given for a personal pension scheme in Chapter 3 by extending the basic rate band for the grossed up personal pension contribution when calculating the tax liability.

Tax relief for an occupational pension scheme

Tax relief for employee contributions to occupational pension schemes is usually given under NET PAY ARRANGEMENTS. This means the employer deducts the contributions from the employee's earnings before he deducts income tax under the PAYE system (as shown above as an allowable deduction).

An employer may also make contributions to a registered pension scheme as part of an employment benefits package. Such contributions are **exempt benefits** for the employee.

Payments from occupational pension schemes to pensioners are made after deduction of income tax under the PAYE system.

Charitable donations under payroll deduction scheme

If an employer has set up a PAYROLL DEDUCTION SCHEME, employees can make tax-deductible donations to an approved charity of their choice by asking the employer to deduct a donation from their gross earnings before deducting income tax under the PAYE system.

This method of making tax deductible donations to charity is sometimes called 'Give As You Earn' or GAYE.

Qualifying travel expenses

Travel expenses are deductible if they are either incurred:

(a) On business travel, or

(b) On travelling from home to a TEMPORARY WORKPLACE. A workplace is temporary if the employee will return to his normal workplace at the end of a temporary period and the temporary period lasts (or is expected to last) for no more than 24 months

Travel from home to a permanent workplace is not allowable.

Approved mileage allowance payments

If an employee uses his own vehicle for business travel, the cost (to the extent that it is not reimbursed) can be claimed as a deduction, under the approved mileage allowance payments scheme (see above).

Expenses incurred wholly, exclusively and necessarily in the performance of the duties of an employment

Expenses incurred **wholly, exclusively and necessarily** in the performance of the duties of an employment are allowable deductions when calculating employment income.

Examples include travelling for business purposes, entertaining customers (see below) and subsistence costs such as meals and hotel expenses.

The test of deductibility is applied quite strictly. For example, none of the cost of renting a phone line is deductible if the phone is also used for private purposes. This is because the line is not used 'exclusively' for business purposes.

Strictly, any other expenses that have a private element are not deductible but, in practice, taxpayers are usually allowed to apportion expenses between parts that are for private purposes and those that are for business purposes. The business part of an expense is deductible.

Reimbursement of expenditure

Sometimes an employee may incur expenditure that is then reimbursed by the employer, such as business entertaining expenditure (see below) or costs of business travel, including staying in hotels. The payment by the employer will be a benefit under the Benefits Code, but the expenditure by the employee may also be an allowable deduction under the rules we have just looked at.

There are two possible treatments of the reimbursement:

(a) The employer may have agreed a **dispensation** with HMRC that the reimbursement and the expenditure by the employee will be ignored for tax purposes

(b) In his employment pages, the employee should include the payment by the employer as a **taxable benefit** but **also** enter his expenditure as an **allowable deduction**. The two entries will cancel each other out to the extent that the expenditure is allowable

Entertaining expenses

The treatment of entertaining expenses in the calculation of employment income depends on how the expense is met by the employer.

Where an employee incurs client entertaining expenses, relief for the expenses will be available to the employee if the expense has been reimbursed by the employer and has been disallowed in arriving at the employer's trading profit.

An employer may provide an employee with a 'round sum allowance', in other words, a fixed monthly sum to cover all employee related expenses. If the employee uses some of this round sum allowance to entertain clients, then the employee will not be able to deduct the client entertaining expenses incurred in arriving at their taxable employment income.

The reason for this restriction is that the employer will have obtained tax relief in full for the payment of the round sum allowance when it is paid to the employee as the employer does not know what the allowance will be spent on. Tax relief is not available for client entertaining so in this situation it is the employee who is penalised for the client entertaining.

In other words, tax relief for entertaining expenses is given either to the employee or the employer, but not both.

EMPLOYMENT TAX PAGE

In your assessment you may have to complete the supplementary employment page that accompanies the income tax return form. A copy of this page is shown below.

HM Revenue & Customs

Employment
Tax year 6 April 2015 to 5 April 2016 (2015-16)

Your name

Your Unique Taxpayer Reference (UTR)

Complete an 'Employment' page for each employment or directorship

1 Pay from this employment – the total from your P45 or P60 - before tax was taken off

£ · 0 0

2 UK tax taken off pay in box 1

£ · 0 0

3 Tips and other payments not on your P60 – read the 'Employment notes'

£ · 0 0

4 PAYE tax reference of your employer (on your P45/P60)

/

5 Your employer's name

6 If you were a company director, put 'X' in the box

6.1 If you ceased being a director before 6 April 2016, put the date the directorship ceased in the box DD MM YYYY

7 And, if the company was a close company, put 'X' in the box

8 If you are a part-time teacher in England or Wales and are on the Repayment of Teachers' Loans Scheme for this employment, put 'X' in the box

Benefits from your employment – use your form P11D (or equivalent information)

9 Company cars and vans - the total 'cash equivalent' amount

£ · 0 0

10 Fuel for company cars and vans - the total 'cash equivalent' amount

£ · 0 0

11 Private medical and dental insurance - the total 'cash equivalent' amount

£ · 0 0

12 Vouchers, credit cards and excess mileage allowance

£ · 0 0

13 Goods and other assets provided by your employer - the total value or amount

£ · 0 0

14 Accommodation provided by your employer - the total value or amount

£ · 0 0

15 Other benefits (including interest-free and low interest loans) - the total 'cash equivalent' amount

£ · 0 0

16 Expenses payments received and balancing charges

£ · 0 0

Employment expenses

17 Business travel and subsistence expenses

£ · 0 0

18 Fixed deductions for expenses

£ · 0 0

19 Professional fees and subscriptions

£ · 0 0

20 Other expenses and capital allowances

£ · 0 0

ℹ Share schemes, employment lump sums, compensation, deductions and Seafarers' Earnings Deduction are on the 'Additional information' pages enclosed in the tax return pack.

SA102 2015   Page E 1   HMRC 12/14

69

BPP
LEARNING MEDIA

HOW IT WORKS

Samantha Sing is employed by Choir plc. The following information relates to her employment:

Annual salary £38,000, with tax deducted of £5,500

Occupational pension contributions (paid by Samantha) £3,000

Company car benefit £4,900

Fuel benefit £2,500

Private medical insurance £250

Professional subscription (paid by Samantha) £175

This would appear on the return as follows:

Name	Samantha Sing
Box 1	35000.00
Box 2	5500.00
Box 5	Choir Plc
Box 9	4900.00
Box 10	2500.00
Box 11	250.00
Box 19	175.00

Assessment focus

In the live assessment you will be provided with 'Taxation Data' that can be accessed through pop-up windows. The content of these taxation data tables has been reproduced at the front of this Text.

The car benefit percentages, fuel benefit and van benefit information covered in this chapter are included within the taxation data pop-up 2 along with the authorised mileage rates and the official rate of interest. Make sure you familiarise yourself with the content and practise referring to it as you work through this Text.

The information included in this chapter typically will be tested in the following tasks:

Task 1 – Benefits in kind – provision of cars

Task 2 – Benefits in kind – all excluding cars

Task 8 – Tax returns

Performance feedback

The assessor's recent comments relevant to this chapter can be summarised as follows:

The vast majority of questions will be computational given the nature of the topic so it is worth noting that less than half of students meet the required standard. Typical errors include not reading the information properly (such as when salaries are given monthly instead of annually); not working out the right number of months; and misreading dates.

Students must read the information carefully – is the car provided for a full year; is it a petrol or diesel engine; is fuel provided; is a contribution made? All these basic areas are routinely being missed by students.

One technical area not covered well by students is contributions made by employees. The distinction between contributions made to the capital cost of the car and monthly contributions to cover the usage of the car is frequently mishandled.

The accommodation questions cause students the most issues.

Rather unusually, the written style questions are better answered than the computational style questions such as explaining deductions from employment income such as professional fees paid privately, pension payments and payroll giving.

The return for employment income tends to be very well handled, the only one recurring error being in Box 1. There is a tendency to either not deduct the occupational pension payment or to add on the PAYE amount.

CHAPTER OVERVIEW

- It is important to distinguish between income from an employment (assessable as employment income) and self-employment (assessable as trading income). The basic question is whether the person is employed under a contract of service, or performs services under a contract for services and is therefore self-employed

- An employee's earnings comprise not only his wages or salary and bonuses, but also employer-provided benefits

- Money earnings are generally received on the earlier of the time payment is made and when the employee becomes entitled to payment. There are special rules for directors

- The taxable benefit arising on a car provided for private use is a percentage of the car's list price

- For cars which emit CO_2 of 0 g/km to 50 g/km the percentage is 5%

- For cars which emit CO_2 from 51 g/km to 75 g/km the percentage is 9%

- For cars which emit CO_2 from 76 g/km to 94 g/km the percentage is 13%

- For cars which emit CO_2 of 95 g/km or more the percentage is 14%, however this percentage increases by 1% for every additional whole 5 g/km of CO_2 emissions above 95 g/km, up to a maximum of 37%

- The percentages are increased by 3% for diesel cars, again up to the maximum of 37%

- The private use of a pool car is an exempt benefit

- There is a taxable benefit of £3,150 a year for private use of a van (but home to work travel is not treated as private use) plus £594 if private fuel is provided

- If the employer provides the employee with assets for private use, there is a taxable benefit each year of 20% of the value of the assets when first provided

- Employer loans written-off give rise to a taxable benefit equal to the loan written-off. For a loan outstanding during the year, there is a taxable benefit equal to the excess of the official rate of interest on the loan over any interest actually charged

- The living accommodation benefit is based on the annual value of the property. An additional benefit arises where the cost of the property exceeds £75,000

- Expenses incurred by the employer in connection with the provision of living accommodation are fully assessable on the employee, unless the employee is in job-related accommodation. In the latter case, the maximum benefit is 10% of the net earnings from the employment

- A deduction from taxable earnings is given to employees for the cost of using their own vehicle for business travel if any mileage allowance paid is less than the statutory rates. Any excess is taxable

- There are certain exempt benefits which are not taxable on employees

- Occupational pension schemes are employer-run schemes. No taxable benefit arises in respect of employer contributions made to pension schemes

- Employee contributions to an occupational pension scheme are deducted from the employee's taxable earnings before tax is applied

- Individuals can make pension contributions up to the higher of:

    (a)   The basic limit (£3,600 – 2015/16)
    (b)   Earnings

- Employees can make charitable donations under an employer's payroll deduction scheme. Such payments are deductible in arriving at taxable earnings

- Employees are generally allowed a deduction for travel costs incurred in the performance of their duties or incurred in travelling to and from home to a temporary workplace. Temporary is taken to be not exceeding 24 months

- For other employment-related expenses to be deductible, such expenses must be 'wholly, exclusively and necessarily' incurred 'in the performance of' the employee's duties

Keywords

The **approved mileage allowance payments scheme** – lays down authorised mileage rates (AMR) at which employees may claim an allowance for business journeys made in their own car

Job-related accommodation – accommodation that is either necessary for the proper performance of duties, or it is for the better performance of the employee's duties and is customarily provided in that type of employment, or is provided as part of special security arrangements

A **temporary workplace** – one at which the employee expects to be for no more than 24 months

Net pay arrangements – where an employer deducts an employee's occupational pension contributions from the employee's earnings before he deducts income tax

A **payroll deduction scheme** – set up by an employer to enable employees to make tax-deductible donations to charity

TEST YOUR LEARNING

Test 1

Someone is regarded as self-employed if he has a contract [~~of~~ *for* service], whereas if he has a contract [under ser], he will be regarded as an employee.

Fill in the missing words.

Test 2

Expenses are deductible in computing taxable earnings if they are incurred [   ] , [   ] and [   ] in the performance of the duties of employment.

Fill in the missing words.

Test 3

Brian uses his own car to travel 8,000 business miles in 2015/16. Brian's employer reimburses him with 35p per mile travelled. The approved mileage rate for the first 10,000 business miles travelled is 45p per mile.

The amounts that are taxable/(deductible) in calculating employment income are (both minus signs and brackets can be used to indicate negative numbers):

£ [(800)]

8 000 × 0,35   2800
8 000 × 0,45   3 600

Test 4

An employee is provided with a flat by his employer (not job-related accommodation). The annual value of the flat is £4,000; rent paid by the employer amounts to £5,900 per annum.

The taxable value of this benefit for 2015/16 is:

£ [5900]

Test 5

A taxable fuel benefit is reduced by any reimbursement by the employee of the cost of fuel provided for private mileage.

TICK ONE BOX.

	✓
True	
False	✓

Test 6

A video recorder costing £500 was made available to Gordon by his employer on 6 April 2014. On 6 April 2015, Gordon bought the recorder for £150, when its market value was £325.

The assessable benefit that arises in 2015/16 is:

£325	
£400	
£175	✓
£250	

Test 7

There is no benefit on the first £10,000 of an interest-free loan.

TICK ONE BOX.

True	✓
False	

Test 8

Gautown was supplied with a petrol engine car by his employer throughout 2015/16. The list price of the car was £24,000 and its CO_2 emissions were 153 g/km.

The taxable benefit arising in respect of the car is:

£ 6000

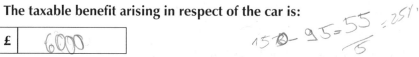

Test 9

Buster is the Managing Director of Buster Braces Ltd and is supplied with a Bentley (three litre, petrol engine) which cost £72,000. It has CO_2 emissions of 165 g/km. All running costs are borne by the company. Buster is also provided with a mobile phone for private and business use. The cost of provision of the phone to Buster Braces Ltd is £750 in 2015/16.

The total taxable benefits are:

£ 26348

Test 10

For each of the following benefits, tick whether they would be taxable or exempt if received by an employee in 2015/16:

Item	Taxable	Exempt
Write off loan of £8,000 (only loan provided)	☑	☐
Payments by employer of £500 per month into registered pension scheme	☐	☑
Provision of one mobile phone	☐	☑
Provision of a company car for both business and private use	☑	☐
Removal costs of £5,000 paid to an employee relocating to another branch	☐	☑
Accommodation provided to enable the employee to spend longer time in the office	☑	☐

chapter 5:
PROPERTY INCOME

---

chapter coverage 📖

In this chapter we first see what property income is and then how to compute the property income that a landlord is taxed on in a tax year. We also look at how losses on lettings are given tax relief.

We then look at the special rules that apply for qualifying holiday accommodation and renting rooms in the taxpayer's main residence (rent a room relief).

We end the chapter by looking at the supplementary land and property pages that must accompany the income tax return form of an individual who has let property in the tax year concerned.

The topics covered are:

- ✍ What is property income?
- ✍ Computing property income
- ✍ Losses
- ✍ Qualifying holiday accommodation
- ✍ Rent a room relief
- ✍ Land and property tax form page

WHAT IS PROPERTY INCOME?

Property income is income that arises from letting out land and buildings. It can include rental income from letting out a piece of land (for example a field for grazing animals), a building such as a house, or part of a building such as a shop or a flat. The person who lets out the land or buildings is called the LANDLORD. The person who occupies the land or buildings is called the TENANT.

In the case of letting out a property in which the tenant lives, the landlord may provide furniture for the tenant to use. This is called a FURNISHED LETTING. If the tenant provides the furniture, the landlord's letting is called an UNFURNISHED LETTING.

COMPUTING PROPERTY INCOME

Property income is taxed as non-savings income (see Chapter 2) on an ACCRUALS BASIS. The accruals basis means that all rental income **accruing ina tax year** is taxed in that year. The date that the income is actually received by the landlord is not relevant.

HOW IT WORKS

Susi bought a property on 6 September 2015. She began letting the property immediately for an annual rent of £36,000 payable in advance in three-monthly instalments due on 6 September, 6 December, 6 March and 6 June.

Rental income is taxed on an accruals basis. This means the income which arises from the letting for the period between 6 September 2015 and 5 April 2016 is taxed in 2015/16. Susi is therefore taxed on £36,000 × 7/12 = £21,000. She actually receives instalments of £9,000 on 6 September, 6 December and 6 March in the tax year, giving total receipts of £27,000, but this is not relevant for the tax calculation.

Expenses incurred by the landlord are also allowed on an accruals basis if they are revenue expenses (rather than capital expenses) that are **wholly and exclusively** incurred for the purpose of letting. Common allowable expenses include:

(a) Advertising for tenants

(b) Accountancy and insurance

(c) Business rates, water rates and council tax

(d) Bad debts if a rent payment appears unlikely to be recoverable, for example if the tenant has left the property owing rent and cannot be traced

(e) Management and agents fees

(f) Maintenance and repair costs such as redecoration

(g) Loan interest and overdraft interest if the related borrowing was applied wholly and exclusively for the purposes of letting the property

Common expenses which are **not allowable** include:

(a) Expenses relating to the landlord's own use of the property

(b) Capital expenses such as the initial cost of the property, installing central heating, construction of walls, extensions, new ensuite bathrooms etc and the cost of furniture (in a furnished letting). The replacement of an item, such as central heating or a fitted kitchen will be treated as a repair (and so allowable) rather than a capital expense provided it is a replacement of a similar standard, not an improvement

HOW IT WORKS

Nadine has let a property unfurnished for many years. She charged rental income of £40,000 for the year to 31 December 2015. The annual rent rose to £44,000 with effect from 1 January 2016.

Expenses relating to the letting were:

	£
Water rates (year to 31 March 2016)	2,000
Insurance (year to 31 December 2015)	600
Insurance (year to 31 December 2016)	800
Agents fees – 10% of rental income	

In June 2015 the tenant accidentally flooded the bathroom. Nadine took the opportunity to strip out the aged bathroom suite and convert the bathroom into a wet room at a total cost of £5,000. This included £900 that was the cost of repairing the flood damage.

Nadine's property income for 2015/16 is:

	£	£
Rental income		
(£40,000 × 9/12) + (£44,000 × 3/12)		41,000
Less: Water rates	2,000	
Insurance (£600 × 9/12) + (£800 × 3/12)	650	
Agents fees (£41,000 × 10%)	4,100	
Repairs	900	
		(7,650)
Taxable property income		33,350

Notes

The rental income and expenses must be dealt with on an accruals basis.

The cost of the flood repairs is allowable because it is a revenue expense. However, the cost of converting the bathroom into a wet room is not allowable because this is a capital expense.

Task 1

Harry owns a nunfurnished property that is let for ten weeks from 1 July 2015 at a rent of £160 per week. The tenants leave at the end of this period having paid only £1,300 of the total amount due. Harry writes-off the outstanding debt because the tenants cannot be traced.

The property is re-let to new tenants on 6 March 2016 for a rent of £400 per month payable in arrears (that means at the end of the month). He received the first payment on 10 April 2016.

He paid interest of £700 during the year ended 5 April 2016 on a loan to purchase the property. The property has been available for letting for the whole tax year.

Harry's taxable rental income for 2015/16 is:

£ [ ]

All letting by an individual landlord is treated as a single source of property income. This means that rents and expenses accruing in a tax year on all let properties must be pooled to arrive at a single figure for property income. The effect of this rule is that if the landlord lets several properties he can set-off the running expenses incurred on empty properties (eg properties between lets), against property income generally.

HOW IT WORKS

Bahrat lets two properties in 2015/16.

Property 1 was bought in June 2015and let unfurnished from 1 July 2015at an annual rent of £18,000 per annum. Buildings insurance of £8,000 was paid for the year to 30 June 2016. £1,200 was spent in June2015on advertising for tenants.

Property 2 became vacant on 5 April 2015. Bahrat then spent £5,000 on repairing the leaking roof in the property. The unfurnished property was let again with effect from 1 March 2016for £24,000 per annum payable monthly in advance. Buildings insurance of £1,800 was incurred for the year to 31 March 2016.

Bahrat's property income for 2015/16 is:

	£	£
Rental income – Property 1		
(9/12 × £18,000)		13,500
Rental income – Property 2		
(1/12 × £24,000)		2,000
Less: Buildings insurance		
– Property 1 (9/12 × £8,000)	6,000	
– Property 2	1,800	
Advertising for tenants	1,200	
Repairs	5,000	
		(14,000)
Taxableproperty income		1,500

Note that a loss would have arisen on Property 2 if it had been dealt with separately. Pooling income and expenses on all let properties effectively allows a loss on one property to be set against income from other properties.

Task 2

Johnson owns two properties which he lets unfurnished as follows:

Whitehouse – let at a rental of £14,000 a year, payable quarterly in advance. The tenant was late in paying the last quarter's rent for the quarter to 5 April 2016 and Johnson did not receive payment until 25 April 2016.

Blackhouse – let at a rental of £6,800 a year payable quarterly in advance. Blackhouse was not let throughout 2015; however, a tenant moved in on 6 January 2016.

Johnson pays agents fees of 15% of rents receivable in respect of both properties to his managing agent. He has also incurred the following expenses:

		Whitehouse £	Blackhouse £
Buildings insurance	– year to 30 June 2015	1,200	980
	– year to 30 June 2016	1,400	1,100
Advertising for tenants		–	450

Johnson's taxable property income for 2015/16 is:

£ _____

Depreciation on plant and machinery used in the letting business is never an allowable expense, as capital allowances (a form of depreciation for tax purposes) are given instead. You will not be expected to compute capital allowances but you may be given a figure for capital allowances that you are expected to deduct in computing the property income.

Capital allowances are not allowed on furniture owned by the landlord and used in a property where the tenant lives (a FURNISHED LETTING). Instead, the landlord obtains relief for such capital expenditure by claiming an allowable expense known as 'the wear and tear allowance'.

The WEAR AND TEAR ALLOWANCE is equal to:

10% [Rents – (Water rates & council tax if paid by the landlord)]

HOW IT WORKS

Polly lets out a furnished property for £8,000 a year. She pays insurance of £300 per annum and water rates of £400 per annum. Polly claims the wear and tear allowance in respect of her furniture. Polly's property income for 2015/16 is:

	£	£
Rental income		8,000
Less: Insurance	300	
Water rates	400	
Wear and tear allowance		
(10% × £(8,000 – 400)	760	
		(1,460)
Property income		6,540

Task 3

Sunita lets out a furnished property for £12,000 per annum. In 2015/16 she pays water rates of £800 and council tax of £900. She also pays an agent's fee of 10% of rent to the agent who manages the letting.

Sunita claims the wear and tear allowance in respect of her furniture.

Sunita's taxable property income for 2015/16 is:

	✓
£8,070	
£7,900	
£9,100	
£9,270	

LOSSES

If a landlord makes an overall loss from the letting of properties, **the property income in that tax year will be Nil.**

The loss is carried forward and set against property income of the following year and subsequent years until the loss is completely used up.

HOW IT WORKS

Maria lets out a house at 30 Thames Drive. Her accrued income and allowable expenses are as follows:

	Income £	Expenses £
2014/15	5,000	12,000
2015/16	7,000	3,000
2016/17	14,000	6,000

The property income for Maria in all three tax years is:

	£
2014/15	
£(5,000 – 12,000) = £(7,000)	
Taxable property income	Nil
2015/16	
£(7,000 – 3,000) = £4,000 less use loss b/f of £(4,000)	
Loss to c/fwd = £(7,000) – £(4,000) used = £(3,000)	
Taxable property income	Nil
2016/17	
£(14,000 – 6,000) = £8,000 less use rest of loss £(3,000)	
Taxable property income	5,000

QUALIFYING HOLIDAY ACCOMMODATION

There are special rules for the taxation of income arising from qualifying holiday accommodation. This can also be referred to as **furnished holiday lettings (FHL).**

Provided certain conditions are satisfied the following **special rules** apply:

(a) The income qualifies as earnings for pension purposes

(b) Capital allowances are available on furniture. The wear and tear allowance isnot available as an alternative

(c)   Losses from furnished holiday lettings can only be carried forward against future profits from the same furnished holiday lettings business. UK losses can relieve UK furnished holiday lettings income only, and similarly with EEA (European Economic Area) losses (see below)

Qualifying holiday accommodation must be:

(a)   Situated in the UK or elsewhere in the EEA; and

(b)   Furnished; and

(c)   Let on a commercial basis with a view to the realisation of profits; and

(d)   Available for letting to the public as holiday accommodation for at least 210 days in the tax year; and

(e)   Actually let for at least 105 days during the same tax year; and

(f)   Not occupied for periods of 'longer-term occupation' (more than 31 consecutive days to the same person) for more than 155 days in a tax year

Where the taxpayer also has other letting income, furnished holiday letting income must be computed separately. UK furnished holiday lettings together comprise one separate business, EEA furnished holiday lettings form another.

It is possible to aggregate the periods of actual letting of more than one property from the same qualifying business to give an average period, ie if one property is let for 100 days and another property is let for 120 days, then the average period of letting for both properties is 110 days which satisfies the 105 day requirement.

The EEA is the European Economic Area and includes all the countries of the European Union (eg France, Spain) and some other European countries (eg Iceland).

Task 4

Joe owns two furnished properties in the UK that he lets out to holidaymakers during 2015/16as follows:

	Property 1	Property 2
Available for letting	200 days	230 days
Actually let	110 days	95days

Which, if any, of his properties will qualify as furnished holiday lettings?

RENT A ROOM RELIEF

To encourage homeowners and tenants to take in lodgers, if an individual lets a furnished room or rooms as living accommodation in his or her main residence, then a special exemption may apply. This is called RENT A ROOM RELIEF. The property must have been the taxpayer's main residence at some point during the tax year.

The individual may own the residence or himself rent it from a landlord. The relief can apply to lettings in a guest house provided that the house in which the business is carried on is also the taxpayer's main residence.

The limit on the relief is income from the provision of accommodation (before any expenses or capital allowances) of **£4,250 a year**. This limit is halved if any other person also receives income from renting accommodation in the property (eg husband and wife). The income to be taken into account includes charges for additional services such as laundry.

If the rental income before expenses is £4,250 a year or less, the rental income is wholly exempt from income tax but the expenses are ignored. However, the taxpayer may elect not to use rent a room relief, for example to make a loss, by taking into account both rent and expenses (ie the ordinary way). The election only applies for the tax year for which it is made. This election must be made by the 31 January that is 22 months from the end of the tax year concerned (ie for the tax year 2015/16, the election must be made by 31 January 2018).

If gross rents exceed £4,250 a year, the taxpayer will be taxed in the ordinary way, ignoring rent a room relief, unless he makes an election to use rent a room relief (the 'alternative basis'). If he makes the election, he will be taxable on gross receipts less £4,250 with no deductions for expenses.

An election to use rent a room relief if gross rents exceed the limit must be made by the 31 January that is 22 months from the end of the tax year concerned. The election remains in force until it is withdrawn or until a year in which gross rents do not exceed the limit.

HOW IT WORKS

Sylvia owns a house near the sea in Norfolk. She has a spare bedroom and during 2015/16 this was let to a chef working at a nearby restaurant for £85 per week, which includes the cost of heating, lighting etc. Sylvia estimates that the extra expenses of these amount to £125 per year.

Gross rents are £4,420 (52 weeks at £85 per week) which exceeds £4,250.

Sylvia has a choice:

(1)   She can be taxed on her actual profit:

	£
Rental income	4,420
Less expenses	(125)
Less wear and tear allowance (10% ×£4,420)	(442)
Taxable property income	3,853

(2)   Elect for rent a room relief (the alternative basis): total rental income is £4,420 which exceeds £4,250 limit so taxable property income is £170 (ie £4,420 – £4,250).

Sylvia should elect to use the rent a room basis as this will give her a lower amount of taxable property income.

Task 5

Jordan and Merry are brother and sister who jointly own a house in which they both live. They rent out one of the rooms to Zach who pays rent of £80 per week which is split equally between Jordan and Merry. The expenses relating to the letting are £400 per year, which includes the wear and tear allowance.

Explain how Jordan and Merry will be taxed in respect of the letting to Zach.

LAND AND PROPERTY TAX FORM PAGE

In your assessment you may be asked to complete the land and property pages that must accompany the income tax return form of someone who lets property. Copies of these pagesare shown below.

The AAT have said that they will only expect students to fill in page 2 of the land and property pages in the assessment, but we have included both pages here for completeness.

 **HM Revenue & Customs**

UK property
Tax year 6 April 2015 to 5 April 2016 (2015-16)

Your name

Your Unique Taxpayer Reference (UTR)

To get notes and helpsheets that will help you fill in this form, go to **www.hmrc.gov.uk/selfassessmentforms**

UK property details

1 Number of properties rented out

2 If all property income ceased in 2015-16 and you do not expect to receive such income in 2016-17, put 'X' in the box and consider if you need to fill in the 'Capital gains summary' page

3 If you have any income from property let jointly, put 'X' in the box

4 If you are claiming Rent a Room relief and your rents are £4,250 or less (or £2,125 if let jointly), put 'X' in the box

Furnished holiday lettings (FHL) in the UK or European Economic Area (EEA)

Please read the 'UK Property notes' before filling in boxes 5 to 19. You need to fill in one page for UK businesses and a separate page for EEA businesses.

5 Income – the amount of rent and any income for services provided to tenants

£ · 0 0

6 Rent paid, repairs, insurance and costs of services provided – the total amount

£ · 0 0

7 Loan interest and other financial costs

£ · 0 0

8 Legal, management and other professional fees

£ · 0 0

9 Other allowable property expenses

£ · 0 0

10 Private use adjustment – read the notes

£ · 0 0

11 Balancing charges – read the notes

£ · 0 0

12 Capital allowances – read the notes

£ · 0 0

13 Adjusted profit for the year (if the amount in box 5 + box 10 + box 11 minus (boxes 6 to 9 + box 12) is positive)

£ · 0 0

14 Loss brought forward used against this year's profits
– if you have a non-FHL property business loss
– read the notes

£ · 0 0

15 Taxable profit for the year (box 13 minus box 14)

£ · 0 0

16 Loss for the year (if the amount in boxes 6 to 9 + box 12 minus (box 5 + box 10 + box 11) is positive)

£ · 0 0

17 Total loss to carry forward

£ · 0 0

18 If this business is in the EEA, put 'X' in the box
– read the notes

19 If you want to make a period of grace election, put 'X' in the box – read the notes

SA105 2015   Page UKP 1   HMRC 12/14

 **BPP** LEARNING MEDIA

89

Property income

Do not include furnished holiday lettings, Real Estate Investment Trust or Property Authorised Investment Funds dividends/distributions here.

20 Total rents and other income from property

£ [   ] · 0 0

21 Tax taken off any income in box 20 - read the notes

£ [   ] · 0 0

22 Premiums for the grant of a lease - from box E on the Working Sheet - read the notes

£ [   ] · 0 0

23 Reverse premiums and inducements

£ [   ] · 0 0

Property expenses

24 Rent, rates, insurance, ground rents etc.

£ [   ] · 0 0

25 Property repairs and maintenance

£ [   ] · 0 0

26 Loan interest and other financial costs

£ [   ] · 0 0

27 Legal, management and other professional fees

£ [   ] · 0 0

28 Costs of services provided, including wages

£ [   ] · 0 0

29 Other allowable property expenses

£ [   ] · 0 0

Calculating your taxable profit or loss

30 Private use adjustment - read the notes

£ [   ] · 0 0

31 Balancing charges - read the notes

£ [   ] · 0 0

32 Annual Investment Allowance

£ [   ] · 0 0

33 Business Premises Renovation Allowance (Assisted Areas only) - read the notes

£ [   ] · 0 0

34 All other capital allowances

£ [   ] · 0 0

35 Landlord's Energy Saving Allowance

£ [   ] · 0 0

36 10% wear and tear allowance - for furnished residential accommodation only - read the notes

£ [   ] · 0 0

37 Rent a Room exempt amount

£ [   ] · 0 0

38 Adjusted profit for the year - from box O on the Working Sheet - read the notes

£ [   ] · 0 0

39 Loss brought forward used against this year's profits

£ [   ] · 0 0

40 Taxable profit for the year (box 38 minus box 39)

£ [   ] · 0 0

41 Adjusted loss for the year - from box O on the Working Sheet - read the notes

£ [   ] · 0 0

42 Loss set off against 2015-16 total income - this will be unusual - read the notes

£ [   ] · 0 0

43 Loss to carry forward to following year, including unused losses brought forward

£ [   ] · 0 0

HOW IT WORKS

Lewis Smith owns an unfurnished property that he rents out throughout 2015/16 for £600 per calendar month, payable in advance. His expenses are as follows:

Water rates £600

Electricity and gas £1,390

Mortgage interest £2,700

Insurance £500

Agent's fees £360

This would appear on the return as follows:

Page 1

Your name: Lewis Smith

Box 1   1

Page 2

Box 20   7200.00 (£600 × 12)

Box24   1100.00 (£600 + £500)

Box26   2700.00

Box27   360.00

Box29   1390.00

Box38   1650.00

Box40   1650.00

Assessment focus

None of the informationin this chapter is included within the 'Taxation Data' which you will be provided with in the live assessment.

The information included in this chapter will typically be tested in the following tasks:

Task 3 – Income from property

Task 8 – Tax returns

Performance feedback

The assessor's recent comments relevant to this chaptercan be summarised as follows:

The property return is the poorest one to be completed and, again, it is attention to detail and reading the information that is necessary. All relevant boxes need to be completed, not just the ones at the top of the return.

With a computational task on income from property, different styles of questions can be expected. Questions may include more than one property. Students can expect both unfurnished and furnished accommodation to be included. Students may need to think carefully about allowable and disallowable expenses.

Students are not performing as well as might be expected in this task which is quite surprising given that it is a straightforward topic area. Perhaps students feel that it is an easy question and are therefore not putting in the work needed to fully understand it. Easy marks are being lost through carelessness and what appears to be rushing answers, so students are advised to take more care.

CHAPTER OVERVIEW

- Property income is income that arises from letting out land and buildings

- Property income accruing in a tax year is taxed in that year

- Property income is calculated by taking the rental income accrued and deducting allowable revenue expenditure accrued

- If an individual lets more than one property, the rents and expenses accruing on all of the let properties are pooled

- A landlord of furnished property may claim the wear and tear allowance

- Losses on rental properties must be carried forward and set against future property profits

- Income from qualifying holiday accommodation counts as earnings for pension purposes

- Capital allowances may be claimed on furniture in qualifying holiday accommodation

- Rent a room relief exempts up to £4,250 of property income when an individual rents a furnished room or rooms in his main residence

Keywords

Landlord – someone who rents out a property to another person

Tenant – the person who occupies the land or building

Furnished letting – a letting which includes the use of furniture belonging to the landlord

Unfurnished letting – is a letting just of the property without furniture

Accruals basis – for taxing rental income means that all rent owing or accruing in a tax year is taxed in that year

Wear and tear allowance – available on furnished properties only and is equal to 10% (rent – water rates – council tax paid by the landlord)

Qualifying holiday accommodation – furnished holiday accommodation let on commercial terms for short periods of time each year with a view to realisation of profit

Rent a room relief – exempts all or part of the property income arising from an individual renting out part of his main residence

TEST YOUR LEARNING

Test 1

David buys a property for letting on 1 August 2015 and grants a tenancy to Ethel from 1 December 2015 at £3,600 pa payable quarterly in advance.

The rental income taxable in 2015/16 is:

£   *1800*

Test 2

Catherine rents out a furnished property for £16,000 pa and pays the water rates of £320 and council tax of £780 on the property.

The wear and tear allowance that Catherine can claim is:

TICK ONE BOX.

1600 - 320 - 780 x 10%

	✓
£1,600	
£1,490	✓
£1,568	
£1,522	

Test 3

John pays buildings insurance premiums for 12 months in advance on 1 October each year to cover all his rental properties. He pays £4,800 in 2014 and £5,200 in 2015.

What amount for building insurance would be allowed against his rental income for 2015/16?

£ [   ]

4800 x 6/12
5200 x 6/12

Test 4

Explain how the loss arising from a furnished holiday let (FHL) can be relieved.

Test 5

Where profits are being made, what is the main income tax advantage of letting qualifying holiday accommodation?

Test 6

Harry owns a property which he lets for the first time on 1 July 2015 at a rent of £4,000 per annum payable monthly in advance.

The first tenants left on 28 February 2016 and the property was re-let to new tenants on 4 April 2016 at a rent of £5,000 per annum payable yearly in advance.

Harry's allowable expenditure was £1,000 in 2015/16.

What is his taxable rental income for 2015/16?

$$4000 \times \frac{8}{12} \quad 2668$$
$$-1000$$
$$5000 \times \frac{1}{12} \quad -417$$

£ | 1667

Test 7

What is the maximum rental income in a tax year which is exempt from income tax under the rent a room scheme?

TICK ONE BOX.

	✓
£2,125	
£4,250	✓
£4,500	
£10,000	

Test 8

Which TWO of the following are not advantages of a property being classed as a furnished holiday let?

	✓
Income can qualify as 'earnings' for pension purposes	
Capital allowances can be claimed on furniture	
Wear and tear allowance can be claimed on furniture	✓
Losses can be set against other income not just property income	✓

chapter 6:
PAYMENT OF TAX AND TAX ADMINISTRATION

chapter coverage 📖

In this chapter we look at when tax returns must be filed, for how long records must be kept, and at the penalties chargeable for failure to comply with the requirements.

We then look at the due dates for payment of income tax and the consequences of late payment.

Finally, we consider HM Revenue & Customs' powers to check tax returns by raising enquiries.

The topics covered are:

✍ Tax returns and keeping records

✍ Penalties

✍ Payment of tax, interest and penalties for late payment

✍ Compliance checks and enquiries

TAX RETURNS AND KEEPING RECORDS

An individual's tax return comprises a Tax Form, together with supplementary pages for particular sources of income and chargeable gains. You may have to complete the supplementary employment or the supplementary land and property pages in your assessment. These forms were included for you to look at earlier in this Text. You will be able to practise completing them in the Personal Tax Question Bank. We will look at chargeable gains and self assessment later in this Text.

Notice of chargeability

Individuals who are chargeable to tax for any tax year and who have not received a notice to file a return are, in general, required to **give notice of chargeability within six months from the end of the tax year**, ie by 5 October 2016 for 2015/16.

Filing tax returns

The FILING DUE DATE is:

(a) For paper returns – the later of:

   (i) **31 October following the end of the tax year** that the return covers, eg for 2015/16, by 31 October 2016

   (ii) **Three months after the issue of the return (see below)**

(b) For returns filed online – the later of:

   (i) **31 January following the end of the tax year** that the return covers, eg for 2015/16, by 31 January 2017

   (ii) **Three months after the issue of the return (see below)**

Where a notice to make a return is issued after 31 July following the tax year, a period of three months is allowed for the filing of a paper return.

Where a notice to make a return is issued after 31 October following the tax year, a period of three months is allowed for the online filing of that return.

An individual may ask HMRC to calculate the tax if a paper return is filed. Where an online return is filed, the tax computation is made automatically.

HOW IT WORKS

Advise the following clients of the latest filing date for their personal tax return for 2015/16 if notice to file the return is received on the following dates and the return is:

(a) Paper
(b) Online

Norma   6 April 2016
Melanie   10 August 2016
Olga   12 December 2016

The latest filing dates are:

	Paper	**Online**
Norma	31 October 2016	31 January 2017
Melanie	9 November 2016	31 January 2017
Olga	11 March 2017	11 March 2017

Task 1

HMRC issued a notice to file a tax return for 2015/16 to Myer on 3 November 2016. She filed this return online on 31 March 2017. State the date by which the return should have been filed:

```



```

Records

In order to complete a tax return or to show that the correct tax has been deducted at source, the taxpayer needs to have records of the income received, tax deducted and expenses incurred. Examples of such records include:

(a) Employment income: money earnings received (Form P60), taxable benefits (Form P11D), invoices for allowable expenses

(b) Property income: tenancy agreements, receipts for rent received and expenses paid

(c) Savings income: statements of interest received

(d) Dividend income: dividend certificates

(e) Capital gains: records of acquisition costs, enhancement costs, disposal costs, disposal proceeds

(f) General: details of Gift Aid donations made and statements of contributions to personal pension schemes

Retention of records

HMRC may require taxpayers and third parties such as tax practitioners to produce records relating to a taxpayer's tax affairs.

In general, records must be retained until the later of:

(a) **One year after the 31 January following the tax year** concerned

(b) **Five years after 31 January following the tax year** concerned if the taxpayer **carries on a business (trading income) or has property income,** for example from renting out a house. In this case, the taxpayer must retain all records relating to the tax year, not just those dealing with the business or letting

HOW IT WORKS

Aleesha is employed by a firm of accountants. She also receives interest on her bank account.

She must retain records relating to income taxable in 2015/16 until 31 January 2018.

Task 2

Michael lets out a house in 2015/16 so has taxable property income for this year. He also receives some dividends from a company.

What is the date until which Michael must retain all his tax records for 2015/16?

PENALTIES

Penalties for errors in the return

A penalty may be imposed where a taxpayer makes an inaccurate return if he has:

(a) **Been careless** because he has not taken reasonable care in making the return or discovers the error later but does not take reasonable steps to inform HMRC

(b) **Made a deliberate error** but does not make arrangements to conceal it

(c) **Made a deliberate error and has attempted to conceal it**, eg by submitting false evidence in support of an inaccurate figure

An error that is made where the taxpayer has taken reasonable care in making the return and which he does not discover later does not result in a penalty.

In order for a penalty to be charged, the inaccurate return must result in:

(a) An understatement of the taxpayer's tax liability; or
(b) A false or increased loss for the taxpayer; or
(c) A false or increased repayment of tax to the taxpayer

If a return contains more than one error, a penalty can be charged for each error. The rules also extend to errors in claims for allowances and reliefs and in accounts submitted in relation to tax liability.

The amount of the penalty for error is based on the Potential Lost Revenue (PLR) to HMRC as a result of the error. For example, if there is an understatement of tax, this understatement will be the PLR.

The maximum amount of the penalty for error depends on the type of error.

A penalty for error may be reduced if the taxpayer tells HMRC about the error – this is called a disclosure. The reduction depends on the circumstances of the disclosure and the help that the taxpayer gives to HMRC in relation to the disclosure.

An unprompted disclosure is one made at a time when the taxpayer has no reason to believe HMRC has discovered, or is about to discover, the error. Otherwise, the disclosure will be a **prompted disclosure**.

The minimum and maximum penalties as percentages of PLR that can be imposed are as follows.

Type of error	Maximum penalty	Minimum penalty with unprompted disclosure	Minimum penalty with prompted disclosure
Mistake	No penalty		
Careless	30%	0%	15%
Deliberate but not concealed	70%	20%	35%
Deliberate and concealed	100%	30%	50%

You will see that an unprompted disclosure where a careless error has been made can reduce a penalty for the error to nil, and all penalties can be reduced by half if the taxpayer makes a prompted disclosure.

A penalty for a careless error may be suspended by HMRC to allow the taxpayer to take action to ensure that the error does not occur again (eg where the error has arisen from failure to keep proper records).

HMRC will impose conditions which the taxpayer has to satisfy, eg establishing proper recordkeeping systems.

The penalty will be cancelled if the conditions imposed by HMRC are complied with by the taxpayer within a period of up to two years.

A taxpayer can appeal against:

(a)   The penalty being charged
(b)   The amount of the penalty
(c)   A decision by HMRC not to suspend a penalty
(d)   The conditions set by HMRC in relation to the suspension of a penalty

---

Task 3

Kitty deliberately omitted savings income in her 2015/16 tax return, but did not destroy the evidence of receipt from the building society. She later disclosed this error, before she had reason to believe HMRC might investigate the matter.

Complete the following sentence:

Kitty's penalty can be reduced from ☐ % of the potential lost revenue (for a deliberate, but not concealed error) to ☐ %, with the unprompted disclosure of her error.

Penalties for late notification

A penalty can be charged for failure to notify chargeability to income tax and/or capital gains tax that results in a loss of tax. Penalties are behaviour related, increasing for more serious failures, and are based on Potential Lost Revenue (PLR). This time the PLR is the income tax or capital gains tax which is unpaid on 31 January following the tax year.

The minimum and maximum penalties as percentages of PLR that can be imposed are as follows:

Behaviour	Maximum penalty	Minimum penalty with unprompted disclosure		Minimum penalty with prompted disclosure	
Deliberate and concealed	100%	30%		50%	
Deliberate but not concealed	70%	20%		35%	
		≥12m	<12m	≥12m	<12m
Careless	30%	10%	0%	20%	10%

There is no zero penalty for reasonable care (as there is for penalties for errors on returns – see above), although the penalty may be reduced to 0% if the failure is rectified within 12 months through unprompted disclosure. The penalties may also be reduced at HMRC's discretion in 'special circumstances'. Inability to pay the penalty is not a 'special circumstance'.

The same penalties apply for failure to notify HMRC of a new taxable activity.

Where the taxpayer's failure is not 'deliberate', there is no penalty if he can show he has a 'reasonable excuse'. Reasonable excuse does not include having insufficient money to pay the penalty. Taxpayers can appeal against penalty decisions.

Penalties for late filing

The penalties for filing a late tax return are:

(a) **Immediate £100 penalty** (even if no tax is owing)

(b) In addition to (a), if the return is more than three months late, **a daily penalty of £10 for each following day may be levied** (up to maximum 90 days)

(c) In addition to (a) and (b), **5% of the tax due** if the return is more than six months but less than 12 months late

(d) In addition to (a), (b) and (c), if the return is more than 12 months late the penalty is

 (i) **100% of the tax due** where withholding of information is **deliberate and concealed,** or

 (ii) **70% of the tax due** where withholding of information is **deliberate but not concealed,** or

 (iii) **5% of the tax due in other cases** (eg careless)

These tax based penalties (c) and (d) above are all subject to a minimum of £300.

Penalties for failure to keep records

The maximum penalty for each failure to keep and retain records is **£3,000** per tax year.

PAYMENT OF TAX, INTEREST AND PENALTIES FOR LATE PAYMENT

Payment of tax

A taxpayer must usually make **three payments of income tax:**

Date	Payment
31 January in the tax year	First payment on account
31 July after the tax year	Second payment on account
31 January after the tax year	Final payment to settle any remaining liability

Each PAYMENT ON ACCOUNT is equal to 50% of the income tax payable (ie after the deduction of tax suffered at source) for the previous year.

Capital gains tax must all be paid on 31 January following the tax year. There are no payments on account of capital gains tax.

HOW IT WORKS

Jeremy paid tax for 2015/16 as follows:

	£
Income tax payable	12,000
Capital gains tax payable	2,000

The payments on account for 2016/17 are:

The income tax payable for 2015/16 was £12,000, therefore each payment on account for 2016/17 is £12,000/2 = £6,000.

Task 4

Karen paid tax for 2015/16 as follows:

	£
Income tax payable	14,000
Capital gains tax payable	8,000

Complete the following:

Each payment on account for 2016/17 will be

£ [   ]

They will be due on

[   ]

and

[   ]

Payments on account are not required if the income tax payable for the previous year is less than £1,000, or if more than 80% of the previous year's liability was paid by tax deducted at source.

Payments on account are normally fixed by reference to the previous year's income tax payable (ie after the deduction of tax suffered at source) but if a taxpayer expects his tax payable to be lower than this, he may claim to reduce his payments on account.

If the taxpayer's eventual tax payable is higher than he estimated (after making such a claim) he will have reduced the payments on account too far. Although the payments on account will not be adjusted, the taxpayer will suffer an interest charge on the underpayments.

The balance of any income tax is normally payable on or before the 31 January following the tax year.

HOW IT WORKS

Jameel made payments on account for 2015/16 of £7,500 each on 31 January 2016 and 31 July 2016, based on his 2014/15 tax payable of £15,000. He later calculates his total income tax payable for 2015/16 at £20,000. He also calculates that the capital gains tax payable for 2015/16 is £4,900.

The final payment for 2015/16, payable on 31 January 2017, is calculated as follows:

	£
Income tax (£20,000 – £7,500 – £7,500)	5,000
Capital gains tax	4,900
Final payment	9,900

The due date for the final payment is normally 31 January following the end of the tax year. However, if the taxpayer has notified chargeability by 5 October but the notice to file a tax return is not issued before 31 October, then the due date for the final payment is three months after the issue of the notice.

Penalties for late payment of tax

Penalties for late payment of tax will be imposed in respect of balancing payments of income tax and any capital gains tax (CGT).

Length of delay	Penalty
(a) Within 30 days of due date:	none
(b) More than 30 days but not more than six months after the due date:	5% of unpaid tax
(c) More than six months but not more than 12 months after the due date:	a further 5% of unpaid tax
(d) More than 12 months after the due date:	a further 5% of unpaid tax

Penalties for late payment of tax **apply to balancing payments** of income tax and any CGT. They **do not apply to late payments on account**.

Interest

INTEREST is chargeable on **late payment of both payments on account and balancing payments**. In both cases interest runs from the **due date until the day before the actual date of payment**.

If a taxpayer claims to reduce his payments on account and there is still a final payment to be made, interest is normally charged on shortfall between the payments on account actually made and the lower of:

(a)   The reduced amount, plus 50% of the final balance of income tax payable

(b)   The amount which would have been payable had no claim for reduction been made

HOW IT WORKS

Harry made two payments on account of £2,500 each for 2015/16. The payments were made on 31 January 2016 and 31 July 2016. Harry had claimed to reduce these payments from the £4,000 that would have been due had they been based on his previous year's income tax payable.

Harry's 2015/16 tax return showed that his tax payable for 2015/16 (before deducting payments on account) were income tax: £10,000; capital gains tax: £3,000. Harry paid the balance of tax due of £8,000 on 30 September 2017.

Harry will be charged interest as follows:

Payments on account would have been £4,000 each if no claim for a reduction had been made. The reduced amount, plus 50% of the final balance of income tax payable is £5,000 (£2,500 + 50% (£10,000 – 2 × £2,500)).

Interest will therefore be charged on the shortfall of £1,500 (£4,000 – £2,500) not paid on 31 January 2016, from that date until the day before payment (29 September 2017). Similarly, interest will run on the other £1,500 that should have been paid on 31 July 2016 until the day before payment, ie 29 September 2017.

The final balancing payment should have been income tax £2,000 (£10,000 – 2 × £4,000) plus capital gains tax £3,000 = £5,000. Interest will run on £5,000 from the due date of 31 January 2017 until the day before payment 29 September 2017.

Note. There would also be a late payment penalty of 10% due on the actual balancing payment of £8,000 (more than six months late).

Repayment of tax and repayment interest

Tax is repaid when claimed unless a greater payment of tax is due in the following 30 days, in which case it is set-off against that payment.

Interest is paid on overpayments of:

(a)   Payments on account
(b)   Final payments of income tax and CGT
(c)   Penalties

REPAYMENT INTEREST runs from the **later of the date of overpayment or the date the tax was due until the day before the tax is repaid**. Tax deducted at source is treated as if it had been paid on the 31 January following the end of the tax year.

COMPLIANCE CHECKS AND ENQUIRIES

HMRC has the power to conduct a compliance check into an individual's tax return.

Some returns are selected for a compliance check at random, others for a particular reason, for example, if HMRC believes that there has been an underpayment of tax due to the taxpayer's failure to comply with tax legislation.

There are **two different types of compliance check:**

(a) Pre-return checks, which are conducted using its information powers

(b) Enquiries into returns, claims or elections which have already been submitted

Examples of when a pre-return check may be carried out in practice include:

(a) To assist with clearances or ruling requests

(b) Where a previous check has identified poor record-keeping

(c) To check that computer systems will produce the information needed to support a return

(d) To find out about planning or avoidance schemes

(e) Where fraud is suspected

Notice must be given by HMRC of the intention to conduct an enquiry by:

(a) The first anniversary of the actual filing date

(b) If the return is filed after the due filing date, the quarter day following the first anniversary of the actual filing date. The quarter days are 31 January, 30 April, 31 July and 31 October

HMRC has only one opportunity to open a formal enquiry and a tax return cannot be subject to a formal enquiry more than once.

In the course of the enquiries the taxpayer may be requested to produce documents, accounts or other information. This request can be made informally or HMRC may issue a written 'information notice'. The taxpayer can appeal to the Tax Tribunal against this.

HMRC must issue a closure notice when the enquiries are complete, state the conclusions and amend the self-assessment accordingly. If the taxpayer is not satisfied with the amendment he may, within 30 days, appeal to the Tax Tribunal.

Assessment focus

None of the information in this chapter is included within the 'Taxation Data' which you will be provided with in the live assessment.

The information included in this chapter will typically be tested in the following task:

Task 7 – Theory underpinning topic and penalties – This topic area will usually be assessed via a free text written response.

Performance feedback

The assessor's recent comments relevant to this chapter can be summarised as follows:

An article was written entitled 'Extended writing tasks – guidance', which is on the AAT website. The guidance given here very much still stands. Students are simply not answering the questions as posed as they lack the skill needed to break down information, digest it, consider it and then appropriately respond.

In order to maximise marks students are advised to use a separate paragraph to tackle each part of a question. For instance the question could ask for penalties for the late return, penalties for late payment of tax and collection of the outstanding tax, so three separate paragraphs would be advised in the answer. By doing this, if one element is answered incorrectly, it will not affect the marks for the other elements as they are distinct.

Students have a tendency to write what they are thinking at the time, irrespective of natural progression through the question. Therefore, it can be very tricky to work out which bit of the question they are answering.

Students also tend to write totally irrelevant information in the answer, possibly to just fill the box. Typical extraneous details would be to write all the tax rates and personal allowances and say that HMRC use this information to calculate the tax liability. If students genuinely do not know the answer, they would benefit from not wasting time on writing this kind of detail, and hence giving themselves more time to use on other tasks.

CHAPTER OVERVIEW

- A tax return must be filed by 31 January following a tax year provided it is filed online. Paper returns must be filed by 31 October following the tax year

- Taxpayers must keep records of income received, tax deducted and expenses paid

- Taxpayers must keep records until the later of:
  - (a) One year after the 31 January following the tax year
  - (b) Five years after the 31 January following the tax year if in business or with property income

- A penalty may be imposed if the taxpayer makes an error in his tax return, based on the Potential Lost Revenue as a result of the error

- A penalty may be imposed if the taxpayer does not notify HMRC of his liability to pay income tax or capital gains tax. The penalty is based on Potential Lost Revenue

- A fixed penalty of £100 applies if a return is filed late; followed by a potential daily penalty of £10 if the return is filed between three and six months late

- A tax-geared penalty will also apply if a return is filed more than six months late, with a further penalty if this is over 12 months late

- Payments on account of income tax are required on 31 January in the tax year and on 31 July following the tax year

- Balancing payments of income tax and all CGT are due on 31 January following the tax year

- Late payment penalties apply to balancing payments of income tax or any CGT. They do not apply to late payments on account

- Interest is chargeable on late payment of both payments on account and balancing payments

- HMRC can enquire into a return, usually within one year of receipt of the return

Keywords

Filing due date – the date by which a return must be filed

Payment on account – an amount paid on account of income tax

Interest – charged on late payments on account and on late balancing payments

Repayment interest – payable by HMRC on overpaid payments on account, balancing payments and penalties

TEST YOUR LEARNING

Test 1

The due filing date for an income tax return for 2015/16 assuming the taxpayer will submit the return online is (insert date as XX/XX/XXXX):

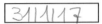 31/1/17

Test 2

Select the correct answers from the drop down lists provided.

The 2015/16 payments on account will be calculated as

 50%. ▼

of the income tax payable for

 2016/15 ▼

and will be due on

 31/1/16 ▼

and

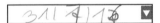 31/7/16 ▼

Picklist 1	Picklist 2	Picklist 3	Picklist 4
50%	2015/16	31 January 2017	31 July 2016
25%	2014/15	31 January 2015	31 July 2015
100%	2016/17	31 January 2016	31 January 2017

Test 3

A notice requiring a tax return for 2015/16 is issued in April 2016 and the return is filed online in May 2017. All income tax was paid in May 2017. No payments on account were due.

Explain what charges will be made on the taxpayer.

Test 4

Sase filed her 2015/16 tax return online on 28 January 2017.

By what date must HMRC give notice that it is going to enquire into the return?

TICK ONE BOX.

	✓
31 January 2018	
31 March 2018	
6 April 2018	
28 January 2018	L—

Test 5

Jamie paid income tax of £12,000 for 2014/15. In 2015/16, his income tax payable was £16,000.

Jamie's 2015/16 payments on account will each be

£  8000 6000

and will be due on (insert date as XX/XX/XXXX)

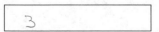 8000

and (insert date as XX/XX/XXXX)

 3

Jamie's balancing payment will be

£  4000

and will be due on (insert date as XX/XX/XXXX)

Test 6

Tim should have made two payments on account of his 2015/16 income tax payable of £5,000 each. He actually made both of these payments on 31 August 2016.

State the amount of any penalties for late payment.

£ | 0

Test 7

Lola accidentally fails to include a sales invoice of £17,000 on her 2015/16 tax return. She pays tax at 40%, and has not yet disclosed this error.

Identify the maximum penalty that could be imposed on her.

TICK ONE BOX.

	✓
£6,800	
£3,400	
£2,040	✓
£1,020	

17,000 × 40 ×

6800 × 30)

chapter 7:
CHARGEABLE GAINS

---
chapter coverage 📖

In this chapter we see how to compute chargeable gains or allowable losses arising on the disposal of assets, including part disposals of assets.

We see how to set allowable losses against chargeable gains and how to arrive at the net gains taxable in any particular tax year. Then we note how to compute the capital gains tax payable in any particular tax year.

We also look at the special rules that apply when disposals are made to connected persons or between married couples/civil partners.

Finally we consider the rules that apply to chattels.

The topics covered are:

- ✍ When does a chargeable gain arise?
- ✍ Computing chargeable gains and allowable losses
- ✍ Part disposals
- ✍ Computing taxable gains in a tax year
- ✍ Computing capital gains tax payable
- ✍ Self assessment for capital gains tax
- ✍ Connected persons
- ✍ Spouses/civil partners
- ✍ Chattels
- ✍ Capital gains summary pages

WHEN DOES A CHARGEABLE GAIN ARISE?

You saw earlier in this Text that, as a general rule, income is a receipt that is expected to recur (such as rental income), whereas a gain arises on a one-off disposal of a capital asset (eg the sale of an investment property for a profit). For the gain on the disposal of a capital asset to be a chargeable gain there must be a CHARGEABLE DISPOSAL of a CHARGEABLE ASSET by a CHARGEABLE PERSON.

Chargeable persons

Individuals are the only type of chargeable person that you will meet in the Personal Tax assessment.

Chargeable disposals

The following are the most important **chargeable disposals:**

(a)   Sales of assets or parts of assets
(b)   Gifts of assets or parts of assets
(c)   The loss or destruction of an asset

A chargeable disposal occurs on the date of the contract (where there is one, whether written or oral), or the date of a conditional contract becoming unconditional.

Exempt disposals include:

(a)   Transfers on death
(b)   Gifts to charities

On death the heirs inherit assets as if they bought them at death for their then market values (known as 'probate value'). There is no capital gain or allowable loss on death.

Chargeable assets

All assets are chargeable assets unless they are specifically designated as exempt.

The following are the **exempt assets** that you need to be aware of:

(a)   Motor vehicles suitable for private use
(b)   Gilt-edged securities (government stock)
(c)   Certain chattels (see later in this chapter)
(d)   Premium bonds
(e)   Investments held in an ISA

Any gain arising on the disposal of an exempt asset is not taxable and any loss is not allowable.

The exempt asset most commonly appearing in assessment questions is a car. You should not waste time computing a gain or loss on a car. All you need to do is state that the car is an exempt asset, so no gain or loss arises.

Task 1

Which of the following are chargeable assets for CGT purposes?

	Chargeable ✓	Exempt ✓
A diamond necklace		
A cash sum invested in premium bonds that results in a substantial win		
A vintage Rolls Royce		

COMPUTING CHARGEABLE GAINS AND ALLOWABLE LOSSES

Whenever a **chargeable asset** is disposed of, a calculation to determine the amount of any gain or loss is needed. The computation follows a standard format as shown below:

	£
Disposal consideration (or market value)	100,000
Less incidental costs of disposal	(1,000)
Net proceeds	99,000
Less allowable costs	(28,000)
Less enhancement expenditure	(1,000)
Chargeable gain	70,000

We will now look at each of the items in the above pro forma in turn.

Disposal consideration

Usually the disposal consideration is the proceeds of sale of the asset, but a disposal is deemed to take place at market value:

(a) Where the disposal is by way of a gift

(b) Where the disposal proceeds are less than market value (known as a 'sale at undervalue' or 'partial consideration')

(c) Where the disposal is made for a consideration which cannot be valued

(d) Where the disposal is made to a connected person (see below)

Costs

The following costs are deducted in the above pro forma:

(a) **Incidental costs of disposal**

These are the costs of selling an asset. They may include advertising costs, estate agents fees, legal costs or valuation fees. These costs should be deducted separately from any other allowable costs.

(b) **Allowable costs**

These include:

(i)   The original purchase price of the asset (or probate value if inherited)
(ii) Costs incurred in purchasing the asset (estate agents fees, legal fees etc)

(c) **Enhancement expenditure**

ENHANCEMENT EXPENDITURE is capital expenditure which enhances the value of the asset and is reflected in the state or nature of the asset at the time of disposal.

Task 2

Jack bought a holiday cottage for £25,000. He paid legal costs of £600 on the purchase.

Jack spent £8,000 building an extension to the cottage.

Jack sold the cottage for £60,000. He paid estate agent's fees of £1,200 and legal costs of £750.

Jack's gain on sale is:

£ [   ]

PART DISPOSALS

Sometimes a part rather than the whole of an asset is disposed of. For instance, one-third of a piece of land may be sold. In this case, we need to be able to compute the chargeable gain or allowable loss arising on the part of the asset disposed of.

The problem is that although we know what the disposal proceeds are for the part of the asset disposed of, we do not usually know what proportion of the 'cost' of the whole asset relates to that part. The solution to this is to **use the following fraction to determine the cost of the part disposed of**.

The fraction is:

$$\frac{A}{A+B} = \frac{\text{Value of the part disposed of}}{\text{Value of the part disposed of} + \text{Market value of the remainder}}$$

A is the 'gross' proceeds (or market value) before deducting incidental costs of disposal.

You must learn the above formula for use in your assessment.

The formula is used to apportion the cost of the whole asset. If, however, any expenditure was incurred wholly in respect of the part disposed of, it should be treated as an allowable deduction in full for that part and not apportioned. An example of this is incidental selling expenses, which are wholly attributable to the part disposed of.

HOW IT WORKS

Mr Jones bought four acres of land for £270,000. He sold one acre of the land at auction for £200,000, before auction expenses of 15%. The market value of the three remaining acres is £460,000.

The cost of the land being sold is:

$$\frac{200,000}{200,000 + 460,000} \times £270,000 = £81,818$$

	£
Disposal proceeds	200,000
Less incidental costs of sale (15% × £200,000)	(30,000)
Net proceeds	170,000
Less cost (see above)	(81,818)
Chargeable gain	88,182

Note that the 'cost' of the land retained is £188,182 (£270,000 − £81,818).

Task 3

Yarrek bought a plot of land for investment purposes for £100,000. In January 2016, he sold part of the land for £391,000, which was net of legal fees on the sale of £9,000. At that time, the value of the remaining land was £600,000.

The chargeable gain arising on the disposal is:

£ [   ]

COMPUTING TAXABLE GAINS IN A TAX YEAR

An individual pays capital gains tax (CGT) on any **taxable gains** arising in a **tax year** (6 April to 5 April). However this is a completely separate computation from that of income tax which we have seen so far in this Text.

All the **chargeable gains** made in the tax year are added together, and any capital losses made in the same tax year are deducted to give net gains (or losses) for the year. Any unrelieved capital losses brought forward from previous years may then be deducted. Finally **the annual exempt amount is deducted to arrive at taxable gains,** on which capital gains tax will be calculated.

A standard format is shown below:

	£
Chargeable gains in tax year	100,000
Less capital losses in tax year	(27,000)
Net gains for the year	73,000
Less capital losses brought forward	(15,000)
Net chargeable gains	58,000
Less annual exempt amount	(11,100)
Taxable gains	46,900

Annual exempt amount

All individuals are entitled to an annual exempt amount. This may also be referred to as an **annual exemption** in your assessment. For 2015/16 the annual exempt amount is £11,100. As you can see above, it is the last deduction to be made in computing taxable gains, and effectively means that for 2015/16 the first £11,100 of chargeable gains are tax-free.

Task 4

In 2015/16 Tina has the following gains:

	£
Chargeable gains	18,100

Tina's taxable gains for 2015/16 are:

£ | 7,000

Losses

Sometimes an allowable loss rather than a taxable gain arises. Once a loss has been calculated, deal with it as follows:

(a) First, set it against gains arising in the same tax year (shown as 'capital losses in the tax year' in the above pro forma) until these are reduced to £Nil, then

(b) Carry any remaining loss forward to set against net gains in the next tax year but only to reduce the net gains in the next tax year down to the level of the annual exempt amount. This means the taxpayer does not lose the benefit of the annual exempt amount. Any loss remaining is carried forward to subsequent tax years and this process repeated until the loss has been relieved.

BPP
LEARNING MEDIA

HOW IT WORKS

(1) Tim has chargeable gains for 2015/16 of £25,000 and allowable losses of £16,000. As the losses are current year losses they must be fully relieved against the gains to produce net gains of £9,000, despite the fact that net gains are below the annual exempt amount. The unused portion of the annual exempt amount is lost.

	£
Chargeable gains in tax year	25,000
Less losses in tax year	(16,000)
Net chargeable gains	9,000
Less annual exempt amount	(11,100)
Taxable gains	Nil

(2) Hattie has gains of £12,000 for 2015/16 and allowable losses brought forward of £6,000. Hattie restricts her loss relief to £900 so as to leave net gains of (£12,000 – £900) = £11,100, which will be exactly covered by the annual exempt amount for 2015/16.

	£
Net chargeable gains	12,000
Less losses brought forward	(900)
	11,100
Less annual exempt amount	(11,100)
Taxable gains	Nil

The remaining £5,100 (£6,000 – £900) of losses will be carried forward to 2016/17.

(3) Mildred has chargeable gains of £2,000 for 2015/16 and losses brought forward from 2014/15 of £12,000. As the gains of £2,000 are covered by the annual exempt amount for 2015/16, there is no need to use any of her brought forward losses, so she will leapfrog 2015/16 completely and carry forward all the brought forward losses to 2016/17.

Task 5

Susan had chargeable gains of £13,100 and allowable losses of £1,000 in 2015/16. She also had allowable losses of £3,000 brought forward from 2014/15.

The capital losses carried forward to 2016/17 are:

	✓
Nil	
£4,000	
£3,000	
£2,000	✓

COMPUTING CAPITAL GAINS TAX PAYABLE

Taxable gains are chargeable to capital gains tax at the rate of 18% or 28% depending on the individual's taxable income for the tax year. If the individual is a basic rate taxpayer then CGT is payable at 18% on the amount of taxable gains up to the amount of the taxpayer's unused basic rate band and at 28% on the excess. If the individual is a higher or additional rate taxpayer then CGT is payable at 28% on all their taxable gains.

HOW IT WORKS

(1) Sally has taxable income (ie the amount after the deduction of the personal allowance) of £10,000 in 2015/16 and made taxable gains (ie gains after deduction of the annual exempt amount) of £20,000 in 2015/16.

The taxable income uses £10,000 of the basic rate band, leaving £21,785 of the basic rate band unused, therefore all of the taxable gain is taxed at 18%.

Sally's capital gains tax liability is therefore:

£20,000 × 18%   £3,600
This is payable on 31 January 2017.

BPP
LEARNING MEDIA

(2) Harry has taxable income of £50,000 in 2015/16 (ie he is a higher rate taxpayer). He made taxable gains of £10,000 in 2015/16.

All of Harry's basic rate band has been taken up by the taxable income, therefore the taxable gain is taxed at 28%.

Harry's capital gains tax liability is therefore:

£10,000 × 28%   £2,800

(3) Isabel has taxable income of £30,000 in 2015/16 and made taxable gains of £25,000 in 2015/16.

Isabel has (£31,785 – £30,000) = £1,785 of her basic rate band unused. Isabel's capital gains tax liability is therefore:

	£
£1,785 × 18%	321
£23,215 × 28%	6,500
£25,000	6,821

Task 6

Sarah made the following chargeable gains and allowable losses in 2015/16.

		£
Gain: 17 July 2015	21000	21,100
Loss: 25 August 2015	⁻4500	(4,500)
Gain: 15 November 2015	+ 17,500	17,500

Sarah pays income tax at the additional rate in 2015/16.

The CGT payable for 2015/16 by Sarah is:

31785

34100 - 31785 = 2315 × 28%

£ 4440

SELF ASSESSMENT FOR CAPITAL GAINS TAX

A taxpayer who makes chargeable gain(s) in a tax year is usually required to file details of the gain(s) in a tax return. In many cases, the taxpayer will be filing a tax return for income tax purposes and will include the capital gains supplementary pages. You will find copies of these at the end of this chapter.

If, however, the taxpayer only has chargeable gains to report, **he must notify his chargeability to HMRC by 5 October following the end of the tax year**. The penalty for late notification is the same as for late notification of income tax chargeability.

The filing date for the tax return is the same as for income tax and the same penalties apply for CGT as for income tax in relation to late filing and errors on the return.

Capital gains tax is payable on 31 January following the end of the tax year. There are no payments on account. The consequences of late payment of CGT are the same as for late payment of income tax so penalties and interest may be charged. Repayment interest may be paid on overpayments of CGT.

CONNECTED PERSONS

If a disposal is made to a connected person, **the disposal proceeds are deemed to be the market value of the asset at the date of disposal**.

If an **allowable loss arises** on the disposal, it can **only be set off against gains** arising in the same or future tax years from disposals **to the same connected person**, and the loss can only be set off if he or she is still connected with the person making the loss.

For this purpose an individual is connected with:

(a)   His relatives (brothers, sisters, lineal ancestors and lineal descendants)
(b)   The relatives of his spouse/civil partner
(c)   The spouses/civil partners of his and his spouse's/civil partner's relatives

---

Task 7

On 1 August 2015 Holly sold a painting to her sister, Emily for £40,000. The market value of the painting on the date of sale was £50,000. Holly had bought the painting for £60,000.

The allowable loss arising on disposal of the painting by Holly is (both minus signs and brackets can be used to indicate negative numbers):

£ | (10,000)

Explain how may this be relieved.

SPOUSES/CIVIL PARTNERS

Spouses/civil partners are taxed as two separate people. Each individual has an annual exempt amount, and allowable losses of one individual cannot be set against gains of the other.

BPP
LEARNING MEDIA

Disposals between spouses/civil partners do not give rise to chargeable gains or allowable losses. The disposal is said to be on a 'NO GAIN/NO LOSS' basis. The acquiring spouse/civil partner takes the costs of the disposing spouse/civil partner (known as the 'base cost').

Task 8

William sold an asset to his wife Kate in May 2015 for £32,000 when its market value was £45,000. William acquired the asset for £14,000 in June 2005.

What is the chargeable gain on this transfer?

	✓
Nil	✓
£18,000	
£31,000	
£13,000	

CHATTELS

A CHATTEL is **tangible moveable property** (ie property that can be moved, seen and touched). Examples are items such as furniture and works of art.

A WASTING CHATTEL is a **chattel with an estimated remaining useful life of 50 years or less**. An example would be a racehorse or a greyhound. **Wasting chattels are exempt from CGT** (so that there are no chargeable gains and no allowable losses). There is one exception to this, being plant and machinery used in the taxpayer's trade, but this is not in your syllabus.

Task 9

Jamie bought a racing greyhound for £6,000. The greyhound was sold for £10,000.

Decide whether the following statement is True or False.

A chargeable gain of £4,000 arises on the disposal.

	✓
True	
False	✓

There are special rules for calculating gains and losses on non-wasting chattels:

(a) If a chattel is not a wasting asset, any gain arising on its disposal will still be exempt from CGT if the asset cost £6,000 or less and it is sold for gross proceeds of £6,000 or less.

(b) If sale proceeds exceed £6,000, but the cost was £6,000 or less, the gain is limited to:

$5/3 \times$ (Gross proceeds – £6,000)

(c) If sale proceeds are less than £6,000, but the asset cost more than £6,000, any allowable loss is restricted to that which would arise if it were sold for gross proceeds of £6,000.

We will have a look at examples of each of these situations in turn.

HOW IT WORKS

John purchased a painting for £3,000. On 1 January 2016 he sold the painting at auction.

If the gross sale proceeds are £4,000, the gain on sale will be exempt.

If the gross sale proceeds are £8,000 with costs of sale of 10%, the gain arising on the disposal of the painting will be calculated as follows:

	£
Gross proceeds	8,000
Less incidental costs of sale (10% × £8,000)	(800)
Net proceeds	7,200
Less cost	(3,000)
Chargeable gain	4,200
Gain cannot exceed 5/3 × £(8,000 – 6,000)	3,333

Therefore the chargeable gain is £3,333.

Task 10

Jacky purchased a non-wasting chattel for £2,500. On 1 October 2015 she sold the chattel at auction for gross proceeds of £10,000 (which was subject to auctioneer's commission of 5%). The gain arising is:

	✓
Nil	
£5,833	
£7,000	
£6,667	✓

(handwritten annotations:)

100,000

10,000 × 5% = 500

99500
− 2500
9,700

10,000 − 6000 × 5/3 = 6666�7

HOW IT WORKS

Magee purchased an antique desk for £8,000. She sold the desk in an auction for £4,750 net of auctioneer's fees of 5% in November 2015.

Magee obviously has a loss but as the proceeds are less than £6,000 (and cost was more than £6,000) the allowable loss is calculated on **deemed proceeds of £6,000**. The costs of disposal can be deducted from the deemed proceeds of £6,000.

	£
Deemed disposal proceeds	6,000
Less incidental costs of disposal (£4,750 × 5/95)	(250)
	5,750
Less cost	(8,000)
Allowable loss	(2,250)

Task 11

Jameel purchased a non-wasting chattel for £8,800 which he sold at auction for £3,600 (which was net of 10% commission).

The allowable loss is (both minus signs and brackets can be used to indicate negative numbers):

£ | (3200)

(handwritten annotations:)

6000
(400)   (3600 × 10/90)

5600
−(8800)

(−3200)

Interaction of chattels and part disposals

When the part disposal rules are applied to the sale of 'part of an asset', the allocation of the cost between the part disposed of and the remaining asset may then result in the need to consider the chattels rules.

HOW IT WORKS

Miguel owned three vases. He had bought these together as a set for £7,500. He sold one of the vases in October 2015 for £9,000. The other two vases were together worth £13,500 at that time. As we know, this is treated as a part disposal of the set.

The gain on sale of one vase

	£
Proceeds	9,000
Less cost (9,000/(9,000 + 13,500)) × £7,500	(3,000)
Gain	6,000

As the apportioned cost is now < £6,000 the chattel rules will be applied:

Gain cannot exceed 5/3 × £(9,000 − 6,000)	5,000

Note. There are special rules that prevent taxpayers splitting up a set of assets and selling them separately in order to use the £6,000 exemption, but these rules are not in your syllabus.

Task 12

In 2015/16, Mr California sold the following chattels.

Chattel	Cost £	Proceeds £
Vase	800	7,000
Sideboard	7,000	5,000

All proceeds are shown before selling expenses of 5% of the gross proceeds. Compute the chargeable gain or allowable loss on each chattel.

CAPITAL GAINS SUMMARY PAGES

In your assessment you may be asked to complete the capital gains summary pages.

The AAT has stated that students can expect to fill in some or all of the capital gains pages in the assessment.

A copy of these pages are shown below.

 **HM Revenue & Customs**

Capital gains summary
Tax year 6 April 2015 to 5 April 2016 (2015-16)

1 Your name

2 Your Unique Taxpayer Reference (UTR)

Summary of your enclosed computations

Please read the 'Capital gains summary notes' before filling in this section. **You must enclose your computations, including details of each gain or loss, as well as filling in the boxes.**

ⓘ To get notes and helpsheets that will help you fill in this form, go to www.hmrc.gov.uk/selfassessmentforms

3 Total gains (boxes 21 + 27 + 33 + 34)

£ · 0 0

4 Gains qualifying for Entrepreneurs' Relief (but excluding gains deferred from before 23 June 2010) - read the notes

£ · 0 0

5 Gains invested under Seed Enterprise Investment Scheme and qualifying for relief - read the notes

£ · 0 0

6 Total losses of the year - enter '0' if there are none

£ · 0 0

7 Losses brought forward and used in the year

£ · 0 0

8 Adjustment to Capital Gains Tax - read the notes

£ · 0 0

9 Additional liability for non-resident or dual resident trusts

£ · 0 0

10 Losses available to be carried forward to later years

£ · 0 0

11 Losses used against an earlier year's gain (special circumstances apply - read the notes)

£ · 0 0

12 Share loss relief used against income - amount claimed against 2015-16 income - read the notes

£ · 0 0

13 Amount in box 12 relating to share loss relief to which Enterprise Investment Scheme/Seed Enterprise Investment Scheme relief is attributable

£ · 0 0

14 Losses used against income - amount claimed against 2014-15 income - read the notes

£ · 0 0

15 Amount in box 14 relating to shares to which Enterprise Investment Scheme/Seed Enterprise Investment Scheme relief is attributable

£ · 0 0

16 Income losses of 2015-16 set against gains

£ · 0 0

17 Deferred gains from before 23 June 2010 qualifying for Entrepreneurs' Relief

£ · 0 0

SA108 2015   Page CG 1   HMRC 12/14

Listed shares and securities

18 **Number of disposals** - read the notes

☐☐☐☐

19 **Disposal proceeds**

£ ☐☐☐☐☐☐☐☐ · 0 0

20 **Allowable costs (including purchase price)**

£ ☐☐☐☐☐☐☐☐ · 0 0

21 **Gains in the year, before losses**

£ ☐☐☐☐☐☐☐☐ · 0 0

22 **If you are making any claim or election, put the relevant code in the box** - read the notes

☐☐☐

23 **If your computations include any estimates or valuations, put 'X' in the box**

☐

Unlisted shares and securities

24 **Number of disposals** - read the notes

☐☐☐☐

25 **Disposal proceeds**

£ ☐☐☐☐☐☐☐☐ · 0 0

26 **Allowable costs (including purchase price)**

£ ☐☐☐☐☐☐☐☐ · 0 0

27 **Gains in the year, before losses**

£ ☐☐☐☐☐☐☐☐ · 0 0

28 **If you are making any claim or election, put the relevant code in the box** - read the notes

☐☐☐

29 **If your computations include any estimates or valuations, put 'X' in the box**

☐

Property and other assets and gains

30 **Number of disposals**

☐☐☐☐

31 **Disposal proceeds**

£ ☐☐☐☐☐☐☐☐ · 0 0

32 **Allowable costs (including purchase price)**

£ ☐☐☐☐☐☐☐☐ · 0 0

33 **Gains in the year, before losses**

£ ☐☐☐☐☐☐☐☐ · 0 0

34 **Attributed gains where personal losses cannot be set off**

£ ☐☐☐☐☐☐☐☐ · 0 0

35 **If you are making any claim or election, put the relevant code in the box** - read the notes

☐☐☐

36 **If your computations include any estimates or valuations, put 'X' in the box**

☐

Any other information

37 **Please give any other information in this space**

SA108 2015   Page CG 2

HOW IT WORKS

Lucy Lane has given you the following information about her capital gains position for 2015/16:

Asset sold	Proceeds	Cost
Antique table	£20,500	£11,000
Listed shares	£12,000	£7,500
Unlisted shares	£9,000	£11,700

She also has losses brought forward from 2014/15 of £1,200

This would appear on the return as follows:

Box 1 (name)	Lucy Lane
Box 3	14000.00
Box 6	2700.00
Box 7	300.00
Box 10	900.00 (1,200 – 300 used)
Box 18	1
Box 19	12000.00
Box 20	7500.00
Box 21	4500.00
Box 24	1
Box 25	9000.00
Box 26	11700.00
Box 27	0.00
Box 30	1
Box 31	20500.00
Box 32	11000.00
Box 33	9500.00

Assessment focus

In the live assessment you will be provided with 'Taxation Data' that can be accessed through pop-up windows. The content of these taxation data tables has been reproduced at the front of this Text.

The annual exempt amount and capital gains tax rates included within this chapter are included within the taxation data pop-up 2. Make sure you familiarise yourself with the content and practise referring to it as you work through this Text.

The information included in this chapter will typically be tested in the following tasks:

Task 8 – Tax returns

Task 9 – Basics of capital gains tax

Task 11 – Capital gains tax exemptions, losses reliefs and tax payable

Performance feedback

The assessor's recent comments relevant to this chapter can be summarised as follows:

The return for the capital gains is reasonably well completed, but more attention to detail is required. All of the return needs completing.

On straightforward capital disposal computations, only 40% of students are meeting the competence level.

Miscellaneous aspects of capital gains computations, mainly being chattels and part disposals, which are relatively straightforward topics, students are struggling to show a solid level of competence.

Part disposals seem to cause the most difficulty with many students simply gaining no marks at all for questions in this topic area. It is hard to see how students find this computation so complex, but the basis of apportioning cost between the part sold and the part retained is a major issue.

Chattels cause less of an issue, but there is evidence of students struggling to accurately apply the relief formula.

The relationship between losses and the annual exempt amount is often assessed, yet students show a lack of full understanding of this relationship.

CHAPTER OVERVIEW

- A chargeable gain/allowable loss arises when there is a chargeable disposal of a chargeable asset by a chargeable person

- Enhancement expenditure can be deducted in computing a chargeable gain/allowable loss if it is reflected in the state and nature of the asset at the time of disposal

- On the part disposal of an asset the formula A/(A + B) must be applied to work out the cost attributable to the part disposed of

- Taxable gains are net chargeable gains for a tax year (ie minus allowable losses of the current tax year and any unrelieved capital losses brought forward) minus the annual exempt amount

- Losses brought forward are used to the extent that they reduce net chargeable gains down to the annual exempt amount

- The rates of CGT are 18% and 28%, but the lower rate of 18% only applies if and to the extent that the individual has any unused basic rate band

- CGT is payable by 31 January following the end of the tax year

- CGT is self assessed and has the same rules about notification of chargeability, penalties and interest as income tax

- A disposal to a connected person uses market value as disposal proceeds

- For individuals, connected persons are broadly brothers, sisters, lineal ancestors and descendants and their spouses/civil partners plus similar relations of a spouse/civil partner

- Losses on disposals to connected persons can only be set against gains on disposals to the same connected person

- Disposals between spouses/civil partners take place on a no gain/no loss basis

- Wasting chattels are exempt assets for CGT purposes (eg racehorses and greyhounds)

- If a non-wasting chattel that cost £6,000 or less is sold for gross proceeds of £6,000 or less, any gain arising is exempt

- If gross proceeds exceed £6,000 on the sale of a non-wasting chattel but the cost is £6,000 or less, any gain arising on the disposal of the asset is limited to 5/3 × (Gross proceeds – £6,000)

- If the gross proceeds are less than £6,000 on the sale of a non-wasting chattel which cost more than £6,000, any loss otherwise arising is restricted by deeming the gross proceeds to be £6,000

Keywords

Chargeable disposal – a sale or gift of an asset

Chargeable asset – any asset that is not an exempt asset

Chargeable person – an individual

Exempt asset – an asset on which no chargeable gain or allowable loss arises

Exempt disposal – a disposal on which no chargeable gain or allowable loss arises

Enhancement expenditure – capital expenditure that enhances the value of the asset and is reflected in the state or nature of the asset at the time of disposal

Taxable gains – the chargeable gains of a tax year, after deducting allowable losses of the same tax year, any unrelieved capital losses brought forward and the annual exempt amount

No gain/no loss disposal – a disposal on which no gain or loss arises

Chattel – tangible moveable property

Wasting chattel – a chattel with an estimated remaining useful life of 50 years or less

TEST YOUR LEARNING

Test 1

Tick to show if the following disposals would be chargeable or exempt for CGT.

	Chargeable ✓	Exempt ✓
A gift of an antique necklace		✓
The sale of a building	✓	

Test 2

Yvette buys an investment property for £325,000. She sells the property on 12 December 2015 for £560,000.

Her chargeable gain on sale is:

£ [   ]

Test 3

Richard sells four acres of land (out of a plot of ten acres) for £38,000 in July 2015. Costs of disposal amount to £3,000. The ten-acre plot cost £41,500. The market value of the six acres remaining is £48,000.

The chargeable gain/allowable loss arising is:

TICK ONE BOX.

	✓
£16,663	✓
£17,500	✗
£19,663	
£18,337	✓

$$\frac{38000}{38000 + 48,000} \times 41,500$$

$$86\,000 \qquad = 18337$$

$$17500$$

$$\begin{array}{r} 38000 \\ -\ 3000 \\ \hline 35000 \\ 18337 \end{array}$$

Test 4

Philip has chargeable gains of £171,000 and allowable losses of £5,300 in 2015/16. Losses brought forward at 6 April 2015 amount to £10,000.

The amount liable to CGT in 2015/16 is:

£ [   ]

handwritten:
171,000
− 5,300
165,700 − 10,000 = 155,700
− 11,100
144,600

The losses carried forward are (both minus signs and brackets can be used to indicate negative numbers):

£ [(450,00)]

Test 5

Martha is a higher rate taxpayer who made chargeable gains (before the annual exempt amount) of £24,000 in October 2015.

Martha's CGT liability for 2015/16 is:

£ [3,612]

handwritten:
24,000
− 11,100
12,900 × 28%

Test 6

A loss arising on a disposal to a connected person can be set against any gains arising in the same tax year or in subsequent tax years.

TICK ONE BOX.

	✓
True	
False	✓

Test 7

No gain or loss arises on a disposal to a spouse/civil partner.

TICK ONE BOX.

	✓
True	√
False	

Test 8

The payment date for capital gains tax for 2015/16 is (insert date as XX/XX/XXXX):

[31/1/17]

Test 9

Complete the table by ticking the appropriate box for each scenario.

	Actual proceeds used	Deemed proceeds (market value) used	No gain or loss basis
Paul sells an asset to his civil partner Joe for £3,600			✓
Grandmother gives an asset worth £1,000 to her grandchild		✓	
Sarah sells an asset to best friend Cathy for £12,000 when it was worth £20,000	✓	✓	

Test 10

Mustafa bought a non-wasting chattel for £3,500.

The gain arising if he sells it for:

(a) **£5,800 after deducting selling expenses of £180 is:**

£ 0

(b) **£8,200 after deducting selling expenses of £220 is:**

£ 4033

8200
+ 220
8420 − 6000 × 5⁄3

Test 11

Simon bought a racehorse for £4,500. He sold the racehorse for £9,000 in December 2014.

The gain arising is:

£ 0

Test 12

Santa bought a painting for £7,000. He sold the painting in June 2015 for £5,000.

6000 − 7000

The loss arising is (both minus signs and brackets can be used to indicate negative numbers):

£ (1000)

chapter 8:
SHARE DISPOSALS

chapter coverage 📖

In this chapter we see how to compute chargeable gains and allowable losses on the disposal of shares.

This is a very important chapter as the computation of gains and losses on the disposal of shares is a key task in your assessment. Shares may be assessed as a long task, so you need to be prepared to set out a computation in the way outlined in this chapter.

The topics covered are:

- ✎ Why special rules are needed for shares

- ✎ Matching rules

- ✎ Share pool

- ✎ Bonus and rights issues

- ✎ Listed and unlisted shares

WHY SPECIAL RULES ARE NEEDED FOR SHARES

Shares present special problems when computing gains or losses on disposal. For instance, suppose that a taxpayer buys some shares in X plc on the following dates:

	No of shares	Cost
		£
5 July 1992	150	195
17 January 1997	100	375
2 July 2015	100	1,000

On 15 June 2015, he sells 220 of his shares for £3,300. **To work out his chargeable gain, we need to be able to identify which shares** out of his three holdings **were actually sold.** Since one share is identical to any other, it is not possible to work this out by reference to factual evidence.

As a result, it has been necessary to devise 'matching rules'. These allow HMRC to identify on a disposal which shares have been sold and so **work out what the allowable cost** (and therefore the gain or loss) **on disposal should be.** These matching rules are considered in detail below.

It is very important that you understand the matching rules. These rules are very regularly assessed and if you do not understand them you will not be able to get any of this part of a task right.

MATCHING RULES

For individuals, when shares are disposed of, the disposal is matched with acquisitions in the following order:

(a) **Shares acquired on the same day as the day of disposal**

(b) **Shares acquired in the 30 days following the day of disposal** (on a FIFO (first in, first out) basis)

(c) **Shares from the share pool.** The share pool includes all shares acquired before the day of disposal, and is explained below

Task 1

Noah acquired shares in Ark Ltd as follows.

2 August 2011	10,000 shares
25 April 2013	10,000 shares
17 June 2015	1,000 shares
19 June 2015	2,000 shares

Noah sold 15,000 shares on 17 June 2015.

Which shares is he selling for capital gains tax purposes?

SHARE POOL

The share pool includes shares acquired up to the day before the disposal on which we are calculating the gain or loss. It grows when an acquisition is made and shrinks when a disposal is made.

The calculation of the share pool value

To compute the value of the share pool, set-up two columns of figures:

(a) The number of shares
(b) The cost of the shares

Each time shares are acquired, both the number and the cost of the acquired shares are added to those already in the pool.

When there is a disposal from the pool, both the number of shares being disposed of, and a cost relating to those shares, are deducted from the pool. The cost of the disposal is calculated as a proportion of total cost in the pool, based on the number of shares being sold.

HOW IT WORKS

Jackie bought 10,000 shares in X plc for £6,000 in August 1995 and another 10,000 shares for £9,000 in December 2007.

She sold 12,000 shares for £26,000 in August 2015.

The share pool is:

	No of shares	Cost £
August 1995 Acquisition	10,000	6,000
December 2007 Acquisition	10,000	9,000
	20,000	15,000
August 2015 Disposal	(12,000)	(9,000)
(12,000/20,000 × £15,000 = £9,000*)		
c/f	8,000	6,000

* If a total of 20,000 shares cost a total of £15,000, then each share has an average cost of 75p (£15,000/20,000). Therefore, the cost of the 12,000 shares being disposed of is 12,000 × 75p = £9,000.

Another way of looking at it is that Jackie is disposing of 60% of the shares in the pool (12,000/20,000 = 60%), therefore she takes 60% of the cost (60% × £15,000 = £9,000).

The gain on the disposal of the shares is therefore:

	£
Proceeds of sale	26,000
Less allowable cost	(9,000)
Chargeable gain	17,000

Task 2

Joraver bought 9,000 shares in Z plc for £4,500 in May 1998. He sold 2,000 shares in August 2007 for £3,500. He then bought a further 5,000 shares for £7,500 in May 2010.

Joraver sold 10,000 shares for £20,000 in January 2016.

The gain on the sale in January 2016 is:

£ [   ]

May 98
Aug 07

May 10

Share   Cost
9000   4500

(2000) (1000)

7000   3500
5 000 7500
12000 11000
(10,000) (9167)

2000   1833

Proc   20,000
Loss cost 9167
Charge   10833

HOW IT WORKS

Tony bought shares in A Ltd as follows.

11 May 2003	14,000 shares for £20,000
9 April 2008	5,000 shares for £12,000
15 June 2015	5,000 shares for £15,000

He sold 18,000 shares for £49,500 on 5 June 2015.

The disposal is matched first against the acquisition in the next 30 days and then against the shares in the share pool as follows.

(1)   Sale of 5,000 shares bought on 15 June 2015
(2)   Sale of 13,000 shares from the share pool

Disposal of 5,000 shares bought on 15 June 2015

	£
Proceeds of sale $\frac{5,000}{18,000} \times £49,500$	13,750
Less allowable cost	(15,000)
Allowable loss	(1,250)

Disposal of 13,000 shares from the share pool

	£
Proceeds of sale $\frac{13,000}{18,000} \times £49,500$	35,750
Less allowable cost (W)	(21,895)
Chargeable gain	13,855

Therefore the net chargeable gain is:

£(13,855 – 1,250)	12,605

Working	No of shares	Cost
		£
11 May 2003 Acquisition	14,000	20,000
9 April 2008 Acquisition	5,000	12,000
	19,000	32,000
5 June 2015 Disposal	(13,000)	(21,895)
(£32,000 × 13,000/19,000 = £21,895)		
c/f	6,000	10,105

[Handwritten annotations at top of page:]
$$\frac{1000}{6000} \times 21600 = 3600$$
$$- 3800$$
$$(200)$$

Task 3

[Handwritten annotations:]
August 05   5000   10,000
April 08   2000   5000
July 15   7000   15000
8000   18000

Eliot acquired shares in K Ltd as follows.

10 August 2005	5,000 shares for £10,000
15 April 2008	2,000 shares for £5,000
25 July 2015	1,000 shares for £3,800
27 July 2015	500 shares for £1,700

Eliot sold 6,000 shares for £21,600 on 25 July 2015.

Calculate the net chargeable gain arising on the disposal by Eliot.

BONUS AND RIGHTS ISSUES

Bonus issues

BONUS SHARES are **additional shares given free to shareholders based on their current holding(s)**. For example, a shareholder may own 2,000 shares. The company makes a bonus issue of 1 share for every 2 shares held (called 1 for 2 bonus issue). The shareholder will then have an extra 1,000 shares, giving him 3,000 shares overall.

Bonus shares are treated as being acquired at the date of the original acquisition of the underlying shares giving rise to the bonus issue.

Since bonus shares are issued at no cost there is **no need to adjust the original cost**. The total cost stays the same, it is merely spread over a greater number of shares therefore reducing the average cost per share.

Rights issues

In a RIGHTS ISSUE, a **shareholder is offered the right to buy additional shares in the company in proportion to the shares he already holds**.

The difference between a bonus issue and a rights issue is that in a rights issue the new shares are paid for. This results in an **adjustment to the original cost**. In effect, it is treated as a normal addition in the share pool.

HOW IT WORKS

Jonah acquired 20,000 shares for £34,200 in T plc in April 2004. There was a 1 for 2 bonus issue in May 2009 and a 1 for 5 rights issue in August 2015 at £1.20 per share.

Jonah sold 30,000 shares for £45,000 in December 2015.

The share pool is constructed as follows:

	No of shares	Cost
		£
April 2004 Acquisition	20,000	34,200
May 2009 Bonus 1 for 2 (1/2 × 20,000 = 10,000)	10,000	–
	30,000	34,200
August 2015 Rights 1 for 5 @ £1.20	6,000	7,200
(1/5 × 30,000 = 6,000 shares × £1.20 = £7,200)		
	36,000	41,400
December 2015 Disposal	(30,000)	(34,500)
(£41,400 × 30,000/36,000 = £34,500)		
c/f	6,000	6,900

The gain on sale is:

	£
Proceeds of sale	45,000
Less allowable cost	(34,500)
Chargeable gain	10,500

Task 4

Dorothy bought 2,000 shares for £10,000 in S Ltd in August 2004. There was a 1 for 1 rights issue at £2.50 in May 2007 and Dorothy took up all her rights issue shares. There was a 1 for 4 bonus issue in September 2010.

Dorothy sold 3,000 shares for £20,000 in October 2015.

Her chargeable gain on sale is:

£ 11,000

August 04   12000   10,000
2000 × (1 × 25   May 07   2000   5000
4000 × 1   Sept 10   4000   15000
        4   7000   —
Oct 15   5000)   15 060
         (3000)   (9 000)
20000   7000   60000
− 900
11,000

LISTED AND UNLISTED SHARES

The capital gains summary pages require you to show gains on listed and unlisted shares separately. There is no difference in the computation of gains.

LISTED SHARES are listed on a Stock Exchange. A listed company will always have the letters plc (public limited company) in its name.

UNLISTED SHARES are not listed on a Stock Exchange. An unlisted company will have either Ltd (Limited) or plc (public limited company) in its name.

You should be told in the assessment whether shares are listed or unlisted if relevant.

Assessment focus

None of the information in this chapter is included within the 'Taxation Data' which you will be provided with in the live assessment.

The information included in this chapter will typically be tested in the following task:

Task 10 – Taxation of shares

Performance feedback

The assessor's recent comments relevant to this chapter can be summarised as follows:

Despite being more complex than most of the other tasks that cover capital gains tax, it overall achieves the highest level of competence in capital gains tax tasks.

All aspects of shares, including bonus issues, rights issues and matching rules can be expected. The biggest problem, as might be expected, is with the matching rules. Students are simply not following the matching at all and are simply producing a pool based on chronological order. Hence the cost of the disposed shares is simply based on shares already bought.

CHAPTER OVERVIEW

- The matching rules for individuals are:
    - Same day acquisitions
    - Next 30 days acquisitions on a FIFO basis
    - Shares in the share pool
- The share pool runs up to the day before disposal
- Bonus issue and rights issue shares are acquired in proportion to the shareholder's existing holding
- The difference between a bonus and a rights issue is that in a rights issue shares are paid for
- Listed shares are listed on a Stock Exchange, unlisted shares are not listed on a Stock Exchange

Keywords

Bonus shares – shares that are issued free to shareholders based on original holdings

Rights issues – similar to bonus issues except that in a rights issue shares must be paid for

Listed shares – shares listed on a Stock Exchange

Unlisted shares – shares not listed on a Stock Exchange

TEST YOUR LEARNING

Test 1

Tasha bought 10,000 shares in V plc in August 1994 for £5,000 and a further 10,000 shares for £16,000 in April 2009. She sold 15,000 shares for £30,000 in November 2015.

Her chargeable gain is:

TICK ONE BOX.

	✓
£15,750	
£11,500	
£17,000	
£14,250	✓

Handwritten working:

Aug 94   10,000   5000
Aprile 209   10,000   16,000
20,000   21,000
Nov 15 (15000)   45750)
5000   5250

30000
- 15,570
14,250

Test 2

In both a bonus issue and a rights issue, there is an adjustment to the original cost of the shares.

TICK ONE BOX.

	✓
True	✓
False	

Test 3

Marcus bought 2,000 shares in X plc in May 2003 for £12,000. There was a 1 for 2 rights issue at £7.50 per share in December 2004. Marcus sold 2,500 shares for £20,000 in March 2016.

His chargeable gain is: May 03

£ [ ]

Test 4

Mildred bought 6,000 shares in George plc in June 2011 for £15,000. There was a 1 for 3 bonus issue in August 2012. Mildred sold 8,000 shares for £22,000 in December 2015.

Her chargeable gain is:

£ [ ]

chapter 9:
PRINCIPAL PRIVATE RESIDENCE

chapter coverage 📖

In this chapter we look at the exemption that is available for any gain that arises on the disposal of an individual's private residence.

The topic covered is:

✍ Private residences

PRIVATE RESIDENCES

A gain arising on the sale of an individual's only or main private residence (PRINCIPAL PRIVATE RESIDENCE) **is exempt from CGT**, providing the taxpayer has occupied (or is deemed to have occupied) the residence throughout his period of ownership. Any loss in this case is not allowable.

Spouses/civil partners are entitled to only one principal private residence between them. This applies even though they are generally taxed independently.

The basic rule is that the gain is wholly exempt where the owner has occupied the whole of the residence throughout his period of ownership. Where occupation has been for only part of the period, the proportion of the gain exempted is:

$$\text{Total gain} \times \frac{\text{Period of occupation}}{\text{Total period of ownership}}$$

The last 18 months of ownership is deemed occupation (and therefore exempt) if, at some time, the residence has been the taxpayer's main residence.

Task 1

Clare bought herself a flat in April 2010 for £80,000. She lived in the flat until December 2014 when she moved to a farmhouse she had bought to be her main residence. The flat was empty until it was sold in March 2016 for £300,000.

Decide whether the following statement is True or False.

The gain arising on the sale is completely exempt.

TICK ONE BOX.

	✓
True	
False	

Deemed occupation

The exempt period of occupation is also deemed to include certain periods of absence, provided the individual had no other main residence at that time and **the period of absence was at some time both preceded by and followed by a period of actual occupation**(not necessarily immediately).

These periods of **deemed occupation** are:

(a) **Any period** (or periods taken together) of absence, **for any reason**, **not exceeding three years**. Where such a period exceeds three years, three years out of the longer period are deemed to be a period of occupation

(b) **Any periods** during which the **owner was required by his employment to live abroad**

(c) **Any period** (or periods taken together) **not exceeding four years** where the owner was:

    (i) **Self-employed and forced to work away from home** (UK and abroad); or

    (ii) **Employed and required to work elsewhere in the UK** (overseas employment is covered by (b) above)

A period of absence may be treated as deemed occupation (and therefore exempt) under the above rules, even if the residence is let while the owner is away.

HOW IT WORKS

Mr A purchased a house for £50,000 on 31 March 1996. He lived in the house until 30 June 1996. He was then sent to work abroad by his employer for five years before returning to the UK to live in the house again on 1 July 2001. He stayed in the house for six months before moving out to live with friends until the house was sold on 31 December 2015 for £150,000.

First work out the total period of ownership:

31 March 1996 to 31 December 2015 = 19 years and 9 months (or 237 months).

Next, decide what periods are chargeable and which are exempt:

		Exempt months	Chargeable months
(i)	1 April 1996 to 30 June 1996	3	–
(ii)	1 July 1996 to 30 June 2001	60	–
(iii)	1 July 2001 to 31 December 2001	6	–
(iv)	1 January 2002 to 30 June 2014	–	150
(v)	1 July 2014 to 31 December 2015	18	–
		87	150

Explanations:

(i) *April 1996 to June 1996.* Actual occupation

(ii) *July 1996 to June 2001.* Covered by the exemption for periods of absence during which the owner is required by his employment to live abroad. The period is both preceded and followed by a period of owner occupation

(iii) *July 2001 to December 2001.* Actual occupation

(iv) *January 2002 to June 2014.* This period is not eligible to be partly covered by the exemption for three years of absence for any reason, as it is not followed by a period of actual occupation

(v) *July 2014 to December 2015.* Covered by the final 18 months exemption

Then calculate the chargeable gain after the exemption has been applied:

	£
Disposal proceeds	150,000
Less cost	(50,000)
Gain before PPR	100,000
Less exempt under PPR provisions	
$\dfrac{87}{237} \times £100,000$	(36,709)
Chargeable gain	63,291

In this example, had Mr A gone straight to live with friends in July 2001 instead of having six months occupation, he would have lost not only the extra six months, but also the period from July 1996 to June 2001, as this period of absence would lose its status of deemed occupation as the property would not have been occupied again by the owner prior to sale.

Task 2

Shammima bought a house on 1 May 2009 for £80,000. She lived in the house until 30 April 2010 when she went to stay with her elderly mother for two years. Shammima returned to the house on 1 May 2012 and lived in it until 31 August 2012. She went to live in a new house she had bought on 1 September 2012.

The first house was sold on 28 February 2016 for £200,000. Calculate the gain arising on disposal of the first house.

More than one residence

An individual may only have one principal private residence at any one time. As mentioned earlier in this chapter, spouses/civil partners may only have one principal private residence between them.

If an individual owns and lives in two properties, he may elect which is to be regarded as his principal private residence for capital gains tax purposes. This election must be made within two years of the second property being used as a residence (usually the date of acquisition) and, if jointly owned, it must be signed by all of the joint owners.

Assessment focus

None of the information in this chapter is included within the 'Taxation Data' which you will be provided with in the live assessment.

The information included in this chapter will typically be tested in the following task:

Task 11 – Capital gains tax exemptions, losses, reliefs and tax payable

Performance feedback

The assessor's recent comments relevant to this chapter can be summarised as follows:

As may be expected, private residence causes the most issues, although basic questions such as the total length of time of ownership is struggled with.

CHAPTER OVERVIEW

- Any gain arising on the disposal of an individual's principal private residence is exempt from CGT if the individual has occupied/deemed to have occupied the property throughout the period of ownership. A loss on disposal is not allowable

- If there have been periods of non-occupation, then part of any gain on disposal may be chargeable

- Certain periods of non-occupation count as periods of deemed occupation

- The last 18 months of ownership always count as a period of occupation if, at some time, the residence has been the taxpayer's main residence

Keywords

Principal private residence – an individual's only or main residence

Deemed occupation – periods during which an individual is treated as having occupied a residence

TEST YOUR LEARNING

Test 1

Provided the property has at some time been the owner's principal private residence, the last .... months of ownership is always an exempt period.

TICK ONE BOX.

	✓
12	
18	
24	
36	

Test 2

Explain three examples of periods of absence from a property which are deemed periods of occupation for the CGT principal private residence exemption.

Test 3

Josephine purchased a house on 1 April 1998 for £60,000 and used it as her main residence until 1 August 2001 when she was sent by her employer to manage the Paris office. She worked and lived in Paris until 31 July 2005. Josephine returned to live in the house on 1 August 2005 but moved out to live in a new house (to be treated as her main residence) on 1 May 2007. The property was empty until sold on 30 November 2015 for £180,000.

Using the proforma below compute the gain on sale.

	£
Proceeds	
Cost	
Gain before PPR exemption	
PPR exemption	
Chargeable gain	

Test 4

Noddy is selling his main residence, which he has owned for 25 years. He lived in the house for the first 14 years of ownership, then for the next five years he was posted abroad by his employer. He never returned to live in the house during the remainder of his period of ownership.

What fraction of his gain will be exempt under the private residence exemption?

TICK ONE BOX.

	✓
20.5/25	
14/25	
15.5/25	
19/25	

ANSWERS TO CHAPTER TASKS

CHAPTER 1   The tax framework

1   The following have the force of law:

	✓
Acts of Parliament	✓
HMRC Statements of practice	
Statutory Instruments	✓
Extra statutory concessions	

2   You should tell Cornelius that under the AAT *Guidelines* on client confidentiality, you cannot provide him with any information on another client without the specific authority of that client.

CHAPTER 2   Taxable income

1   The total amount of interest to be included in his income tax computation is:

£	260

Building society interest £160 × 100/80 = £200

Plus Treasury Stock interest = £60

2   The gross amount of dividends to be included in her income tax computation is:

£	1,000

(£900 × 100/90)

and the gross amount of interest to be included in her income tax computation is:

£	2,000

(£1,600 × 100/80)

3   The total amount taxable on Denis is:

	✓
£280	✓
£500	
£100	
£680	

NatWest deposit account interest

£80 × 100/80 = £100

Plus Treasury Stock interest = £180

Dividends from shares held within a ISA are exempt from income tax.

4

	Non-savings income £	Savings income £	Dividend income £	Total £
Business income	44,000			
Building society interest		2,000		
Dividends			1,000	
Net income	44,000	2,000	1,000	47,000

Lotto winnings are exempt from income tax.

5

	Non-savings income £	Savings income £	Dividend income £	Total £
Trade profits	11,160			
Building society interest (× 100/80)		2,500		
Dividends (× 100/90)			5,000	
Net income	11,160	2,500	5,000	18,660
Less personal allowance	(10,600)			(10,600)
Taxable income	560	2,500	5,000	8,060

Premium bond prizes are exempt from income tax.

6 The personal allowance that Zelda is entitled to in 2015/16 is:

£	8,100

	Non-savings income £	Savings income £	Dividend income £	Total £
Employment income	97,500			
Bank interest (× 100/80)		5,000		
Dividends (× 100/90)			2,500	
Net income	97,500	5,000	2,500	105,000

	£
Net income	105,000
Less income limit	(100,000)
Excess	5,000
Personal allowance	10,600
Less half excess (5,000/2)	(2,500)
Adjusted personal allowance	8,100

7 Ernest is entitled to a personal allowance in 2015/16 of:

£	6,350

	£
Net income	109,000
Less gross Gift Aid donation	(500)
Adjusted net income	108,500
Less income limit	(100,000)
Excess	8,500
Personal allowance	10,600
Less half excess (8,500/2)	(4,250)
Adjusted personal allowance	6,350

8 The age allowance that Zebedee is entitled to in 2015/16 is:

£ | 10,600

	Non-savings Income £	Savings income £	Dividend income £	Total £
Pension income	21,000			
Bank interest (× 100/80)		2,500		
Dividends (× 100/90)			5,000	
Net income	21,000	2,500	5,000	28,500

	£
Net income	28,500
Less income limit	(27,700)
Excess	800
Age allowance	10,660
Less half excess	(400)
Adjusted age allowance	10,260

But cannot be reduced below £10,600 (unless net income is above £100,000).

CHAPTER 3   Calculation of income tax

1   Her income tax liability is:

£	17,643

	Non-savings income £	Savings income £	Total £
Taxable income	25,000	35,000	60,000

	£
Tax on non-savings income	
£25,000 × 20%	5,000
Tax on savings income (£31,785 – £25,000) = £6,785	
£6,785 × 20%	1,357
£28,215 × 40%	11,286
£60,000	
Income tax liability	17,643

2   Stacey's income tax liability is:

£	60,018

	£
Tax on non-savings income	
£31,785 × 20%	6,357
£78,215 × 40%	31,286
£110,000	
Tax on dividend income	
£40,000 × 32.5%	13,000
£150,000	
£25,000 × 37.5%	9,375
£175,000	
Income tax liability	60,018

3   Joe's income tax liability for 2015/16 is:

£ | 1,224

	Non-savings income £	Savings income £	Total £
Employment income	11,160		
Bank interest (£8,000 × 100/80)		10,000	
Net income	11,160	10,000	21,160
Less personal allowance	(10,600)		(10,600)
Taxable income	560	10,000	10,560

Tax on non-savings income	
£560 × 20%	112
Tax on savings income	
£(5,000 – 560) = £4,440 × 0%	0
£(10,000 – 4,440) = £5,560 × 20%	1,112
Income tax liability	1,224

4   Hans' income tax liability for 2015/16 is:

£ | 12,243

	Non-savings income £	Savings income £	Total £
Taxable income	24,000	26,000	50,000

Tax on non-savings income	
£24,000 × 20%	4,800
Tax on savings income	
£7,785 (£31,785 – £24,000) × 20%	1,557
£7,000 (£5,600 × 100/80) × 20%	1,400
£11,215 × 40%	4,486
£50,000	12,243

Note. The basic rate band is extended by the gross amount of the personal pension contribution paid.

5 The tax payable is:

£	0

	Dividend income £
Dividends (× 100/90)	25,000
Less personal allowance	(10,600)
Taxable income	14,400

	£
Tax on dividend income	
£14,400 × 10%	1,440
Less tax credit on taxable dividend (£14,400 × 10%)	(1,440)
Tax payable	Nil

6

	Non-savings income £	Savings income £	Dividend income £	Total £
Rental income	30,600			
Bank interest (× 100/80)		10,000		
Dividends (× 100/90)			12,000	
Net income	30,600	10,000	12,000	52,600
Less personal allowance	(10,600)			(10,600)
Taxable income	20,000	10,000	12,000	42,000
Tax on non-savings income				
£20,000 × 20%				4,000
Tax on savings income				
£10,000 × 20%				2,000
Tax on dividend income				
£1,785 £(31,785 – 20,000 – 10,000) × 10%				179
£10,215 × 32.5%				3,320
42,000				
Income tax liability				9,499
Less: tax credit on dividend (£12,000 × 10%)				(1,200)
tax suffered on interest (£10,000 × 20%)				(2,000)
Income tax payable				6,299

7

	Non-savings Income £	Savings income £	Total £
Employment income	16,115		
Building society interest (× 100/80)		5,000	
Net income	16,115	5,000	21,115
Less age allowance	(10,660)		(10,660)
Taxable income	5,455	5,000	10,455

	£
Tax on non-savings income	
£5,455 × 20%	1,091
Tax on savings income	
£5,000 × 20%	1,000
Tax liability	2,091
Less: tax deducted from employment income (given)	(1,100)
tax suffered on building society interest (£5,000 × 20%)	(1,000)
Tax repayable	(9)

Note that as Kate was born before 6 April 1938, she is entitled to the higher age allowance of £10,660 instead of the standard personal allowance of £10,600.

Note also that both tax suffered on building society interest and tax suffered on employment income are deducted from the tax liability to arrive at tax payable. As these amounts have exceeded the tax liability, the excess can be repaid.

CHAPTER 4　Employment income

1

Factor	Contract of service	Contract for services
Leon must accept further work if offered	✓	
Leon hires his own helpers		✓
Leon is entitled to paid holidays	✓	
Leon can profit from sound management		✓

2　Rio's earnings for 2015/16 are:

£	20,625

6 April 2015 – 31 December 2015: £20,000 × 9/12 = £15,000
1 January 2016 – 5 April 2016: £22,500 × 3/12 = £5,625
Earnings = £15,000 + £5,625

The bonus is received when Rio becomes entitled to it, which is in the following tax year (2016/17). It is not linked to the period during which it was earned (the company's period of account).

3　Rita receives the bonus on:

	✓
31 December 2015	
31 March 2016	
10 April 2016	✓
15 June 2016	
31 July 2016	
31 October 2017	

This is the date when the amount is determined (which is after the date the company's period of account ends).

4 The taxable benefit on the provision of the car in 2015/16 is:

£	2,400

The CO_2 emissions of the car are 185g/km (rounded down to the nearest five below)

Amount over baseline figure: 185 – 95 = 90g/km

Divide 90 by 5 = 18

The taxable percentage is 14% + 18% = 32%

So the benefit is 32% × £10,000 × 9/12 = £2,400

Note. The benefit is multiplied by 9/12 as the car was only available for nine months in the tax year from 6 July 2015 to 5 April 2016.

5 The total taxable benefit arising to Nissar in 2015/16 is:

£	15,630

Round down CO_2 emissions to 160 g/km

Amount above baseline: 160 – 95 = 65 g/km

Divide 65 by 5 = 13

Taxable % = 14% + 13% + 3% (diesel) = 30%

	£
Car benefit £30,000 × 30%	9,000
Fuel benefit £22,100 × 30%	6,630
Total benefit	15,630

Note. No deduction is made in respect of the amount paid towards the cost of private fuel.

6 The taxable benefit for use arising in 2014/15 is:

£	1,200

Use benefit: £6,000 × 20%

In 2015/16 is:

£	300

Use benefit: £6,000 × 20% × 3/12 (6 April 2015 to 5 July 2015)

The taxable benefit on Ahmed's acquisition in 2015/16 is:

£	3,500

Acquisition	£	£
(a) Market value at acquisition	4,000	–
(b) Market value when first provided	–	6,000
Less assessed in respect of use		
£(1,200 + 300)	–	(1,500)
	4,000	4,500

Take higher, = £4,500

Less amount paid	(1,000)
	3,500

7   The taxable benefit arising in respect of the loan in 2015/16 assuming no elections are made is:

£ | 321

$$\frac{£11,200 + £10,200}{2} \times 3\%$$

As no elections are made, the 'average' method of valuing the loan is used.

8   The total taxable benefit is:

£ | 2,800

Interest: no benefit because loan not over £10,000.

Loan written-off: £8,000 × 35% = taxable benefit.

9   The taxable value of the accommodation provided in 2015/16 is:

	✓
£3,750	
£8,950	✓
£20,950	
£15,750	

	£
Annual value	5,200
Additional benefit £(600,000 – 75,000) × 3%	15,750
	20,950
Less rent paid by Marak	(12,000)
Taxable benefit	8,950

10 Mr Quinton's taxable employment income for 2015/16 is:

£	29,540

	£	£
Salary (= net earnings)		27,400
Accommodation benefits		
Annual value: exempt (job-related)		
Ancillary services		
Electricity	550	
Gas	400	
Gardener	750	
Redecoration	1,800	
	3,500	
Restricted to 10% of £27,400	2,740	
Less employee's contribution (12 × £50)	(600)	
		2,140
Employment income		29,540

11

£	40

	£	£
Amount received 12,000 × 42p		5,040
Less statutory limit		
10,000 × 45p	4,500	
2,000 × 25p	500	
		(5,000)
Taxable benefit		40

12

£	(2,000)

	£	£
Amount received 12,000 × 25p		3,000
Less statutory limit		
(10,000 × 45p)	4,500	
(2,000 × 25p)	500	
		(5,000)
Allowable deduction		(2,000)

CHAPTER 5   Property income

1   Harry's taxable rental income for 2015/16 is:

£ | 1,000

	£
Rental income (net of bad debt)	1,300
Rental income (£400 × 1)	400
Less interest	(700)
Taxable property income	1,000

2   Johnson's taxable property income for 2015/16 is:

£ | 10,475

	£	£
Rental income: Property 1 (accrued)		14,000
Property 2 (3/12 × £6,800)		1,700
		15,700
Less Agent's fees		
(15% × £15,700)	2,355	
Insurance on Whitehouse		
(3/12 × £1,200) + (9/12 × £1,400)	1,350	
Insurance on Blackhouse		
(3/12 × £980) + (9/12 × £1,100)	1,070	
Advertising for tenants	450	
		(5,225)
Taxable property income		10,475

3 Sunita's taxable property income for 2015/16 is:

	✓
£8,070	✓
£7,900	
£9,100	
£9,270	

	£	£
Rental income		12,000
Less: Water rates	800	
Council tax	900	
Agents fees (10% × £12,000)	1,200	
Wear and tear allowance		
10% × £(12,000 – 800 – 900)	1,030	
		(3,930)
Taxable property income		8,070

4 Neither property qualifies.

Property 1 is not available for let for the qualifying 210 days, and Property 2 is not actually let for the qualifying 105 days. The 105 day test is also failed on average ((110 + 95)/2 < 105 days).

5 Jordan and Merry each receive rental income of £(80 × 52)/2 = £2,080. They each have a rent a room limit of £2,125. Since the rental is less than the limit, the rent is wholly exempt from income tax for them. The expenses are ignored. It is possible to elect to ignore rent a room relief but this will not be beneficial in this case.

CHAPTER 6 Payment of tax and tax administration

1   2 February 2017

Since the notice to file was issued after 31 October 2016, the filing date is three months after the notice was issued.

2   31 January 2022

Since Michael has property income the records must be retained for five years after 31 January following the tax year.

3   Kitty's penalty can be reduced from 70 % of the potential lost revenue (for a deliberate, but not concealed error) to 20 %, with the unprompted disclosure of her error.

4   Each payment on account for 2016/17 will be

£ 7,000

Payments on account $\dfrac{£14,000}{2}$

No payments on account are due in respect of CGT.

They will be due on

31 January 2017   (31 January in the tax year 2016/17)

and

31 July 2017   (31 July after the tax year 2016/17)

CHAPTER 7   Chargeable gains

1

	Chargeable ✓	Exempt ✓
A diamond necklace	✓	
A cash sum invested in premium bonds that results in a substantial win		✓
A vintage Rolls Royce		✓

2   Jack's gain on sale is:

£ | 24,450

	£
Proceeds of sale	60,000
Less costs of disposal (£1,200 + £750)	(1,950)
Net proceeds of sale	58,050
Less: original cost	(25,000)
costs of acquisition	(600)
enhancement expenditure	(8,000)
Chargeable gain	24,450

3   The chargeable gain arising on the disposal is:

£ | 351,000

	£
Proceeds of sale (£391,000 + £9,000)	400,000
Less costs of disposal	(9,000)
Net proceeds of sale	391,000
Less cost	
$\dfrac{£400,000}{£400,000+£600,000} \times £100,000$	(40,000)
Chargeable gain	351,000

4   Tina's taxable gains for 2015/16 are:

£ | 7,000

(Chargeable gains of £18,100 less the annual exempt amount of £11,100)

5 The capital losses carried forward to 2016/17 are:

	✓
Nil	
£4,000	
£3,000	
£2,000	✓

2015/16	£
Chargeable gains	13,100
Less allowable losses	(1,000)
	12,100
Less capital losses b/f	(1,000)
Net gains to be covered by the annual exempt amount	11,100

Losses c/f £2,000 (£3,000 b/fwd less £1,000 used in 2015/16)

6 The CGT payable for 2015/16 by Sarah is:

£	6,440

	£
Chargeable gains (£21,100 + £17,500)	38,600
Less allowable loss	(4,500)
	34,100
Less annual exempt amount	(11,100)
Taxable gains	23,000
CGT payable	
£23,000 × 28%	6,440

7 The allowable loss arising on disposal of the painting by Holly is:

£	(10,000)

	£
Deemed proceeds (market value)	50,000
Less cost	(60,000)
Allowable loss	(10,000)

The loss may only be set against gains arising on the disposal of other assets by Holly to Emily in 2015/16 or future tax years.

8

	✓
Nil	✓
£18,000	
£31,000	
£13,000	

William transfers the asset to his wife Kate on a 'no gain/no loss' basis. This assumes that William sold it for 'deemed proceeds' equal to his original cost ie £14,000. The market value and the actual proceeds received are not relevant.

9

	✓
True	
False	✓

No chargeable gain/allowable loss arises as greyhounds are wasting chattels and therefore exempt assets for CGT purposes.

10 The gain arising is:

	✓
Nil	
£5,833	
£7,000	
£6,667	✓

	£
Gross proceeds	10,000
Less commission (5% × £10,000)	(500)
	9,500
Less cost	(2,500)
	7,000

Maximum gain: 5/3 × £(10,000 − 6,000) = £6,667

11 The allowable loss is:

£	(3,200)

	£
Deemed proceeds	6,000
Less commission (£3,600 × 10/90)	(400)
	5,600
Less cost	(8,800)
Allowable loss	(3,200)

12 (a)

The vase	£
Proceeds	7,000
Less selling expenses (£7,000 × 5%)	(350)
	6,650
Less cost	(800)
Chargeable gain	5,850

The gain is the lower of £5,850 and £(7,000 − 6,000) × 5/3 = £1,667, so it is £1,667.

(b)

The sideboard	£
Proceeds (deemed)	6,000
Less selling expenses (£5,000 × 5%)	(250)
	5,750
Less cost	(7,000)
Allowable loss	(1,250)

CHAPTER 8   Share disposals

1   Noah will match his disposal of 15,000 shares on 17 June 2015 as follows:

(1)   1,000 shares bought on 17 June 2015 (same day)

(2)   2,000 shares bought on 19 June 2015 (next 30 days, FIFO basis)

(3)   12,000 shares from the 20,000 shares in the share pool

2   The gain on the sale in January 2016 is:

£ | 10,833

Share pool

	No of shares	Cost
		£
May 1998 Acquisition	9,000	4,500
August 2007 Disposal	(2,000)	(1,000)
(£4,500 × 2,000/9,000 = £1,000)		
c/f	7,000	3,500
May 2010 Acquisition	5,000	7,500
	12,000	11,000
January 2016 Disposal	(10,000)	(9,167)
(£11,000 × 10,000/12,000 = £9,167)		
c/f	2,000	1,833

Gain:

	£
Proceeds of sale	20,000
Less cost	(9,167)
Chargeable gain	10,833

3   Eliot will match the disposal of 6,000 shares on 25 July 2015 as follows:

(1)   1,000 shares bought on 25 July 2015 (same day)

(2)   500 shares bought on 27 July 2015 (next 30 days, FIFO basis)

(3)   4,500 shares from the 7,000 shares in the share pool

Disposal of 1,000 shares bought on 25 July 2015

	£
Proceeds of sale $\frac{1,000}{6,000}$ × £21,600	3,600
Less cost	(3,800)
Allowable loss	(200)

Disposal of 500 shares bought on 27 July 2015

	£
Proceeds of sale $\dfrac{500}{6,000} \times £21,600$	1,800
Less allowable cost	(1,700)
Chargeable gain	100

Disposal of 4,500 shares from the share pool

	£
Proceeds of sale $\dfrac{4,500}{6,000} \times £21,600$	16,200
Less allowable cost (W)	(9,643)
Chargeable gain	6,557

The net chargeable gain is therefore:
£(100 + 6,557 – 200) = £6,457

Working

	No. of shares	Cost £
10 August 2005 Acquisition	5,000	10,000
15 April 2008 Acquisition	2,000	5,000
	7,000	15,000
25 July 2015 Disposal	(4,500)	(9,643)
(£15,000 × 4,500/7,000 = £9,643)		
c/f	2,500	5,357

4 Her chargeable gain on sale is:

£	11,000

	£
Proceeds of sale	20,000
Less allowable cost (W)	(9,000)
Chargeable gain	11,000

Working

Share pool	No. of shares	Cost
		£
August 2004 Acquisition	2,000	10,000
May 2007 Rights issue 1 for 1 @ £2.50	2,000	5,000
(1/1 × 2,000 = 2,000 shares × £2.50 = £5,000)		
c/f	4,000	15,000
September 2010 Bonus 1 for 4	1,000	–
(1/4 × 4,000 = 1,000 shares)		
c/f	5,000	15,000
October 2015 Disposal	(3,000)	(9,000)
(£15,000 × 3,000/5,000 = £9,000)		
c/f	2,000	6,000

CHAPTER 9   Principal private residence

1

	✓
True	✓
False	

Clare was in actual occupation from April 2010 to December 2014.

The last 18 months of ownership are exempt because Clare had previously lived in the flat as her only or main residence. Therefore this covers her period of absence from December 2014 to March 2016.

2   Total period of ownership: 1 May 2009 to 28 February 2016 = 6 years and 10 months (or 82 months).

	Actual or deemed occupation months	Non-occupation months
1 May 2009 to 30 April 2010	12	
1 May 2010 to 30 April 2012	24	
(up to 3 years any reason)		
1 May 2012 to 31 August 2012	4	
1 September 2012 to 31 August 2014		24
1 September 2014 to 28 February 2016	18	
	58	24

	£
Sale proceeds	200,000
Less cost	(80,000)
Gain	120,000
Less PPR £120,000 × 58/82	(84,878)
Chargeable gain	35,122

TEST YOUR LEARNING – ANSWERS

CHAPTER 1 The tax framework

1   All taxpayers are sent a tax return each year by HM Revenue and Customs.

	✓
True	
False	✓

Most taxpayers have all their tax deducted at source and are not sent a tax return.

2   When is a tax practitioner not bound by the ethical Guidelines of client confidentiality?

	✓
When in a social environment	
When discussing client affairs with third parties with the client's proper and specific authority	✓
When reading documents relating to a client's affairs in public places	
When preparing tax returns	

3   Who should a sole practitioner make a report to if he suspects a client of money laundering?

	✓
HMRC	
Nearest police station	
National Crime Agency	✓
Tax Tribunal	

4 The tax administration within the UK is undertaken by:

	✓
The Chancellor of the Exchequer	
Companies House	
HM Revenue & Customs	✓
Members of Parliament	

CHAPTER 2 Taxable income

1 Classify the following types of income by ticking the correct box:

	Non-savings income	Savings income	Dividend income
Employment income	✓	☐	☐
Dividends	☐	☐	✓
Property income	✓	☐	☐
Bank interest	☐	✓	☐
Pension income	✓	☐	☐
Interest on government stock	☐	✓	☐

2 Complete the table below to show the amount of income that would be included in a tax return for 2015/16. If your answer is zero please put a '0'.

	Amount received £	Amount in tax return £
Building society interest (£240 × 100/80)	240	300
Interest on an individual savings account	40	0
Dividends (£144 × 100/90)	144	160
Interest from government gilts	350	350

3   In 2015/16 Joe has employment income of £30,000, receives dividends of £270 and premium bond winnings of £500.

Use the table below to show his taxable income for 2015/16.

	Non-savings income £	Dividend income £	Total £
Employment income	30,000		
Dividends (£270 × 100/90)		300	
Net income	30,000	300	30,300
Less personal allowance	(10,600)		(10,600)
Taxable income	19,400	300	19,700

Premium bond winnings are exempt from income tax.

4   Pratish receives property income of £3,000 and building society interest of £7,200 in 2015/16.

Use the table below to show his taxable income for 2015/16.

	Non-savings income £	Savings income £	Total £
Property income	3,000		
Building society interest			
(£7,200 × 100/80)		9,000	
Net income	3,000	9,000	12,000
Less personal allowance	(3,000)	(7,600)	(10,600)
Taxable income	Nil	1,400	1,400

The personal allowance is deducted first from non-savings income and then from savings income.

5   Jesse has employment income of £112,200 in 2015/16. He also received building society interest of £4,000, a prize of £50 in an internet competition and dividends of £3,600.

Use the table below to show Jesse's taxable income for 2015/16.

	Non-savings income £	Savings income £	Dividend income £	Total £
Employment income	112,200			
Building society interest (× 100/80)		5,000		
Dividends (× 100/90)			4,000	
Net income	112,200	5,000	4,000	121,200
Less personal allowance (W)	(Nil)			(Nil)
Taxable income	112,200	5,000	4,000	121,200

Working

	£
Net income	121,200
Less income limit	(100,000)
Excess	21,200
Personal allowance	10,600
Less half excess	(10,600)
Adjusted personal allowance	Nil

The prize is exempt from income tax.

6   **The age allowance available to Zoreen for 2015/16 is:**

£ | 10,600

Working

	Non-savings income £	Savings income £	Dividend income £	Total £
Pension income	20,380			
Bank interest (× 100/80)		5,000		
Dividends (× 100/90)			6,000	
Net income	20,380	5,000	6,000	31,380

	£
Net income	31,380
Less income limit	(27,700)
Excess	3,680
Age allowance	10,660
Less half excess	(1,840)
	8,820
But cannot be less than	10,600

7   **The tax credit attached to a dividend can be offset against a taxpayer's tax liability, and if it exceeds the liability the taxpayer can receive a repayment.**

	✓
True	
False	✓

The tax credit attached to a dividend can be offset against a taxpayer's tax liability, but if it exceeds the liability the taxpayer cannot receive a repayment.

CHAPTER 3   Calculation of income tax

1   **At what rates is income tax charged on non-savings income?**

	✓
0%, 20%, 40% and 45%	
40% and 45%	
20% only	
20%, 40% and 45%	✓

2   In 2015/16 Albert has a salary of £16,600, £2,000 (gross) of building society interest and £3,000 (gross) of dividends.

Albert's income tax liability is:

£	1,900

Working

	Non-savings income £	Savings income £	Dividend income £	Total £
Net income	16,600	2,000	3,000	21,600
Less personal allowance	(10,600)	–	–	(10,600)
Taxable income	6,000	2,000	3,000	11,000

	£
Tax on non-savings income	
£6,000 × 20%	1,200
Tax on savings income	
£2,000 × 20%	400
Tax on dividend income	
£3,000 × 10%	300
Tax liability	1,900

The £3,000 of dividend income falls within the basic rate band so is taxed at 10%.

3 In 2015/16 Carol has a salary of £5,000, and has received building society interest of £14,400 and a dividend of £19,800.

Carol's income tax liability is:

£	4,269

Working

	Non-savings income £	Savings income £	Dividend income £	Total £
Employment income	5,000			
Interest (× 100/80)		18,000		
Dividends (× 100/90)			22,000	
Net income	5,000	18,000	22,000	45,000
Less personal allowance	(5,000)	(5,600)		(10,600)
Taxable income	Nil	12,400	22,000	34,400

	£
Tax on savings income	
£5,000 × 0%	0
£7,400 × 20%	1,480
£12,400	
Tax on dividend income	
£19,385 × 10%	1,939
£31,785	
£2,615 × 32.5%	850
£34,400	
Income tax liability	4,269

4 In 2015/16 Harry has a salary of £140,000, and has received building society interest of £16,000 and dividends of £27,000.

Harry's income tax liability is:

£ | 69,393

Working

	Non-savings income £	Savings income £	Dividend income £	Total £
Employment income	140,000			
Interest (× 100/80)		20,000		
Dividends (× 100/90)			30,000	
Net income	140,000	20,000	30,000	190,000
Less personal allowance	(Nil)			(Nil)
Taxable income	140,000	20,000	30,000	190,000

The personal allowance is reduced to nil because the net income is so high.

	£
Tax on non-savings income	
£31,785 × 20%	6,357
£108,215 × 40%	43,286
£140,000	
Tax on savings income	
£10,000 × 40%	4,000
£150,000	
£10,000 × 45%	4,500
£160,000	
Tax on dividend income	
£30,000 × 37.5%	11,250
£190,000	
Income tax liability	69,393

5 Basic rate tax relief is obtained by paying Gift Aid donations net of 20% tax. Further tax relief is given to higher and additional rate taxpayers by extending the basic rate band by the gross amount of the Gift Aid donation.

6 **Doreen's income tax payable for the year:**

	Non-savings income £	Savings income £	Dividend income £	Total £
Pension income	17,000			
Property income	3,500			
Interest (received gross)		380		
Dividends (× 100/90)			700	
Net income	20,500	380	700	21,580
Less age allowance	(10,660)			(10,660)
Taxable income	9,840	380	700	10,920

Premium bond prizes are exempt from income tax.

	£
Tax on non-savings income	
£9,840 × 20%	1,968
Tax on savings income	
£380 × 20%	76
Tax on dividend income	
£700 × 10%	70
	2,114
Less tax credit on dividends (£700 × 10%)	(70)
tax deducted from pension income (given)	(2,010)
Income tax payable	34

7 **Sase's income tax payable for the year:**

	Non-savings income £	Savings income £	Dividend income £	Total £
Business profits	36,600			
Building society interest (× 100/80)		5,000		
Dividends (× 100/90)			4,000	
Net income	36,600	5,000	4,000	45,600
Less personal allowance	(10,600)			(10,600)
Taxable income	26,000	5,000	4,000	35,000

	£
Tax on non-savings income	
£26,000 × 20%	5,200
Tax on savings income	
£5,000 × 20%	1,000
Tax on dividend income	
£785 × 10% (£31,785 – 26,000 – 5,000)	79
£2,000 (extended) × 10%	200
£1,215 × 32.5% (£4,000 – 785 – 2,000)	395
Income tax liability	6,874
Less tax credit on dividends (£4,000 × 10%)	(400)
tax suffered on interest (£5,000 × 20%)	(1,000)
Income tax payable	5,474

8   Vince is a higher rate taxpayer and makes a Gift Aid donation of £15,000 in 2015/16.

What is Vince's basic rate band in 2015/16?

£46,785	
£31,785	
£43,785	
£50,535	✓

Working

£15,000 × 100/80 = £18,750 + £31,785

CHAPTER 4   Employment income

1   Someone is regarded as self-employed if he has a contract | for services | , whereas if he has a contract | of service | , he will be regarded as an employee.

2   Expenses are deductible in computing taxable earnings if they are incurred | wholly | , | exclusively | , and | necessarily | in the performance of the duties of employment.

3   Brian uses his own car to travel 8,000 business miles in 2015/16. Brian's employer reimburses him with 35p per mile travelled. The approved mileage rate for the first 10,000 business miles travelled is 45p per mile.

The amounts that are taxable/(deductible) in calculating employment income are:

£	(800)

Working

	£
Amount received: 8,000 × 35p	2,800
Less statutory limit: 8,000 × 45p	(3,600)
Deductible amount	(800)

4   An employee is provided with a flat by his employer (not job-related accommodation). The annual value of the flat is £4,000; rent paid by the employer amounts to £5,900 per annum.

The taxable value of this benefit for 2015/16 is:

£	5,900

being the higher of the annual value and rent actually paid by the employer.

5   **A taxable fuel benefit is reduced by any reimbursement by the employee of the cost of fuel provided for private mileage.**

	✓
True	
False	✓

There is a taxable fuel benefit unless the employer is fully reimbursed for private fuel.

6   A video recorder costing £500 was made available to Gordon by his employer on 6 April 2014. On 6 April 2015, Gordon bought the recorder for £150, when its market value was £325.

The assessable benefit that arises in 2015/16 is:

	✓
£325	
£400	
£175	
£250	✓

Working

The benefit is the higher of:

	£	£
(a) Current MV	325	
(b) Original MV	500	
Less already assessed (in 2014/15)		
£500 × 20%	(100)	
	400	
ie		400
Less amount paid		(150)
Taxable benefit		250

7   **There is no benefit on the first £10,000 of an interest-free loan.**

	✓
True	
False	✓

Only if total loans do not exceed £10,000 at any time in the tax year are they ignored.

8   Gautown was supplied with a petrol engine car by his employer throughout 2015/16. The list price of the car was £24,000 and its CO_2 emissions were 153 g/km.

The taxable benefit arising in respect of the car is:

£ | 6,000

Working

CO_2 emissions = 150 g/km (rounded down)

Above baseline: 150 – 95   = 55 g/km

Divide by 5   =   55/5   = 11

Percentage   =   14% + 11%   = 25%

Benefit 25% × £24,000   = £6,000

9   Buster is the Managing Director of Buster Braces Ltd and is supplied with a Bentley (three litre, petrol engine) which cost £72,000. It has CO_2 emissions of 165 g/km. All running costs are borne by the company. Buster is also provided with a mobile phone for private and business use. The cost of provision of the phone to Buster Braces Ltd is £750 in 2015/16.

The total taxable benefits are:

£ | 26,348

	£
Car benefit (W)	20,160
Fuel benefit (£22,100 × 28%)	6,188
Telephone benefit (exempt – one mobile phone)	Nil
Total benefit	26,348

Working

Amount of emissions above baseline: 165 – 95 = 70 g/km
Divide 70 by 5 = 14
Percentage = 14% + 14% = 28%
£72,000 × 28% = £20,160

10 **For each of the following benefits, tick whether they would be taxable or exempt if received by an employee in 2015/16:**

Item	Taxable	Exempt
Write off loan of £8,000 (only loan provided)	✓	☐
Payments by employer of £500 per month into registered pension scheme	☐	✓
Provision of one mobile phone	☐	✓
Provision of a company car for both business and private use	✓	☐
Removal costs of £5,000 paid to an employee relocating to another branch	☐	✓
Accommodation provided to enable the employee to spend longer time in the office	✓	☐

CHAPTER 5   Property income

1 David buys a property for letting on 1 August 2015 and grants a tenancy to Ethel from 1 December 2015 at £3,600 pa payable quarterly in advance.

The rental income taxable in 2015/16 is:

£	1,200

Rent accrued 1 December 2015 to 5 April 2016 = 4/12 × £3,600

2 Catherine rents out a furnished property for £16,000 pa and pays the water rates of £320 and council tax of £780 on the property.

The wear and tear allowance that Catherine can claim is:

	✓
£1,600	
£1,490	✓
£1,568	
£1,522	

10% × £(16,000 – 320 – 780)

3 John pays buildings insurance premiums for 12 months in advance on 1 October each year to cover all his rental properties. He pays £4,800 in 2014 and £5,200 in 2015.

What amount for building insurance would be allowed against his rental income for 2015/16?

£	5,000

Working

Insurance premiums accrued in 2015/16:

	£
6/12 × £4,800 (6 April 2015 to 30 September 2015)	2,400
6/12 × £5,200 (1 October 2015 to 5 April 2016)	2,600
	5,000

4 Losses from furnished holiday lettings can only be carried forward against future profits from the same furnished holiday lettings business.

5 The income qualifies as earnings for pension purposes. Primarily this gives scope for relief for higher pension contributions.

6 Harry owns a property which he lets for the first time on 1 July 2015 at a rent of £4,000 per annum payable monthly in advance.

The first tenants left on 28 February 2016 and the property was re-let to new tenants on 4 April 2016 at a rent of £5,000 per annum payable yearly in advance.

Harry's allowable expenditure was £1,000 in 2015/16.

What is his taxable rental income for 2015/16?

£	1,667

Working

	£
Rental income (£4,000 × 8/12)	2,667
Less expenses	(1,000)
Taxable rental income	1,667

Rent of £5,000 paid 4 April 2016 accrues in 2016/17 and is therefore taxed in that year.

7   **What is the maximum rental income in a tax year which is exempt from income tax under the rent a room scheme?**

	✓
£2,125	
£4,250	✓
£4,500	
£10,000	

8   **Which TWO of the following are not advantages of a property being classed as a furnished holiday let?**

	✓
Income can qualify as 'earnings' for pension purposes	
Capital allowances can be claimed on furniture	
Wear and tear allowance can be claimed on furniture	✓
Losses can be set against other income not just property income	✓

CHAPTER 6   Payment of tax and tax administration

1   **The due filing date for an income tax return for 2015/16 assuming the taxpayer will submit the return online is (insert date as XX/XX/XXXX):**

> 31/01/2017

2   The 2015/16 payments on account will be calculated as

> 50%

of the income tax payable for

> 2014/15

and will be due on

> 31 January 2016

and

> 31 July 2016

BPP LEARNING MEDIA

3   A notice requiring a tax return for 2015/16 is issued in April 2016 and the return is filed online in May 2017. All income tax was paid in May 2017. No payments on account were due.

Explain what charges will be made on the taxpayer.

£100 penalty for failure to file the return on time (ie by 31 January 2017).

Possible £10 per day penalty from 1 May 2017 (three months after the due filing date) until date of filing.

5% penalty on tax paid late (after 30 days of due date).

Interest on tax paid late.

4   Sase filed her 2015/16 tax return online on 28 January 2017.

By what date must HMRC give notice that it is going to enquire into the return?

	✓
31 January 2018	
31 March 2018	
6 April 2018	
28 January 2018	✓

A year after the actual filing date because Sase filed the return before the due filing date (31 January 2017).

5   Jamie paid income tax of £12,000 for 2014/15. In 2015/16, his income tax payable was £16,000.

Jamie's 2015/16 payments on account will each be

£	6,000

and will be due on (insert date as XX/XX/XXXX)

31/01/2016

and (insert date as XX/XX/XXXX)

31/07/2016

Jamie's balancing payment will be

£	4,000

and will be due on (insert date as XX/XX/XXXX)

31/01/2017

6   Tim should have made two payments on account of his 2015/16 income tax payable of £5,000 each. He actually made both of these payments on 31 August 2016.

State the amount of any penalties for late payment.

£	0

No penalties for late payment are due on late payments on account.

7   Lola accidentally fails to include a sales invoice of £17,000 on her 2015/16 tax return. She pays tax at 40%, and has not yet disclosed this error.

Identify the maximum penalty that could be imposed on her.

	✓
£6,800	
£3,400	
£2,040	✓
£1,020	

Working

Careless error – maximum penalty is 30% × PLR
PLR = £17,000 × 40% = £6,800
30% × £6,800 = £2,040

CHAPTER 7   Chargeable gains

1   **Tick to show if the following disposals would be chargeable or exempt for CGT.**

	Chargeable ✓	Exempt ✓
A gift of an antique necklace	✓	
The sale of a building	✓	

2   Yvette buys an investment property for £325,000. She sells the property on 12 December 2015 for £560,000.

Her chargeable gain on sale is:

£	235,000

Working

	£
Proceeds	560,000
Less cost	(325,000)
Chargeable gain	235,000

3   Richard sells four acres of land (out of a plot of ten acres) for £38,000 in July 2015. Costs of disposal amount to £3,000. The ten-acre plot cost £41,500. The market value of the six acres remaining is £48,000.

The chargeable gain/allowable loss arising is:

	✓
£16,663	✓
£17,500	
£19,663	
£18,337	

Working

	£
Proceeds	38,000
Less costs of disposal	(3,000)
	35,000
Less £41,500 × $\dfrac{38,000}{38,000 + 48,000}$	(18,337)
Chargeable gain	16,663

4   Philip has chargeable gains of £171,000 and allowable losses of £5,300 in 2015/16. Losses brought forward at 6 April 2015 amount to £10,000.

The amount liable to CGT in 2015/16 is:

£	144,600

The losses carried forward are:

£	0

Working

	£
Gains	171,000
Less current year losses	(5,300)
	165,700
Less losses b/f	(10,000)
	155,700
Less annual exempt amount	(11,100)
Taxable gains	144,600

5   Martha is a higher rate taxpayer who made chargeable gains (before the annual exempt amount) of £24,000 in October 2015.

Martha's CGT liability for 2015/16 is:

£	3,612

Working

	£
Chargeable gains	24,000
Less annual exempt amount	(11,100)
Taxable gains	12,900
CGT on £12,900 @ 28%	3,612

6   **A loss arising on a disposal to a connected person can be set against any gains arising in the same tax year or in subsequent tax years.**

	✓
True	
False	✓

A loss on a disposal to a connected person can be set only against gains arising on disposals to the same connected person.

7   **No gain or loss arises on a disposal to a spouse/civil partner.**

	✓
True	✓
False	

8   **The payment date for capital gains tax for 2015/16 is (insert date as XX/XX/XXXX):**

31/01/2017

9 **Complete the table by ticking the appropriate box for each scenario.**

	Actual proceeds used	Deemed proceeds (market value) used	No gain or loss basis
Paul sells an asset to his civil partner Joe for £3,600			✓
Grandmother gives an asset worth £1,000 to her grandchild		✓	
Sarah sells an asset to best friend Cathy for £12,000 when it was worth £20,000		✓	

10 Mustafa bought a non-wasting chattel for £3,500.

The gain arising if he sells it for:

(a) £5,800 after deducting selling expenses of £180 is:

£ | Nil

There is no gain as the chattel cost £6,000 or less and is sold for gross proceeds of £6,000 or less (£5,800 + £180 = £5,980).

(b) £8,200 after deducting selling expenses of £220 is:

£ | 4,033

Working

	£
Gross proceeds	8,420
Less selling expenses	(220)
Net proceeds	8,200
Less cost	(3,500)
	4,700

Gain cannot exceed 5/3 (8,420 – 6,000) = £4,033

Therefore, gain is £4,033

11 Simon bought a racehorse for £4,500. He sold the racehorse for £9,000 in December 2014.

The gain arising is:

£ | Nil

A racehorse is an exempt asset as it is a wasting chattel, so no chargeable gain or allowable loss arises.

12 Santa bought a painting for £7,000. He sold the painting in June 2015 for £5,000.

The loss arising is:

| £ | (1,000) |

Working

	£
Deemed proceeds	6,000
Less cost	7,000)
Allowable loss	(1,000)

CHAPTER 8   Share disposals

1   Tasha bought 10,000 shares in V plc in August 1994 for £5,000 and a further 10,000 shares for £16,000 in April 2009. She sold 15,000 shares for £30,000 in November 2015.

Her chargeable gain is:

	✓
£15,750	
£11,500	
£17,000	
£14,250	✓

Working

	No. of shares	Cost
	£	£
August 1994 Acquisition	10,000	5,000
April 2009 Acquisition	10,000	16,000
	20,000	21,000
November 2015 Disposal	(15,000)	(15,750)
(£21,000 × 15,000/20,000 = £15,750)		
c/f	5,000	5,250

	£
Proceeds of sale	30,000
Less allowable cost	(15,750)
Chargeable gain	14,250

2   **In both a bonus issue and a rights issue, there is an adjustment to the original cost of the shares.**

	✓
True	
False	✓

In a rights issue, shares are paid for and this amount is added to the original cost. In a bonus issue, shares are not paid for and so there is no adjustment to the original cost.

3   Marcus bought 2,000 shares in X plc in May 2003 for £12,000. There was a 1 for 2 rights issue at £7.50 per share in December 2004. Marcus sold 2,500 shares for £20,000 in March 2016.

His chargeable gain is:

£	3,750

Working

	No. of shares	Cost £
May 2003 Acquisition	2,000	12,000
December 2004 1 for 2 rights issue @ £7.50	1,000	7,500
(1/2 × 2,000 = 1,000 shares × £7.50 = £7,500)		
	3,000	19,500
March 2016 Disposal	(2,500)	(16,250)
(£19,500 × 2,500/3,000)		
c/f	500	3,250

	£
Proceeds of sale	20,000
Less allowable costs	(16,250)
Chargeable gain	3,750

4   Mildred bought 6,000 shares in George plc in June 2011 for £15,000. There was a 1 for 3 bonus issue in August 2012. Mildred sold 8,000 shares for £22,000 in December 2015.

Her chargeable gain is:

£	7,000

Working

	No. of shares	Cost
		£
June 2011 Acquisition	6,000	15,000
August 2012 1 for 3 bonus issue	2,000	Nil
(1/3 × 6,000 = 2,000 shares)		
	8,000	15,000
December 2015 Disposal (ie all the shares)	(8,000)	(15,000)
c/f	Nil	Nil

	£
Proceeds of sale	22,000
Less allowable costs	(15,000)
Chargeable gain	7,000

CHAPTER 9   Principal private residence

1   Provided the property has at some time been the owner's principal private residence, the last .... months of ownership is always an exempt period.

	✓
12	
18	✓
24	
36	

2   Explain three examples of periods of absence from a property which are deemed periods of occupation for the CGT principal private residence exemption.

The last 18 months of ownership is deemed occupation if, at some time, the residence has been the taxpayer's main residence.

Providing the taxpayer actually occupies the property both at some point before and at some point after the period of absence, the following periods are deemed occupation for the purpose of PPR exemption:

(a) Periods of up to three years for any reason. Where a period of absence exceeds three years, three years out of the longer period are deemed to be a period of occupation

(b) Periods during which the owner was required by his employment to live abroad

(c) Period of up to four years where the owner was:

    (i) Self-employed and forced to work away from home (UK and abroad)

    (ii) Employed and required to work elsewhere in the UK (overseas employment is covered by (b) above)

3   Josephine purchased a house on 1 April 1998 for £60,000 and used it as her main residence until 1 August 2001 when she was sent by her employer to manage the Paris office. She worked and lived in Paris until 31 July 2005. Josephine returned to live in the house on 1 August 2005 but moved out to live in a new house (to be treated as her main residence) on 1 May 2007. The property was empty until sold on 30 November 2015 for £180,000.

Using the pro forma below compute the gain on sale.

	£
Proceeds	180,000
Cost	(60,000)
Gain before PPR exemption	120,000
PPR exemption 127/212 × £120,000	(71,887)
Chargeable gain	48,113

Working

Total period of ownership: 1 April 1998 to 30 November 2015 = 17 years and 8 months (212 months)

	Exempt months	Chargeable months
1 April 1998 to 31 July 2001 (actual occupation)	40	
1 August 2001 to 31 July 2005 (employed abroad)	48	
1 August 2005 to 30 April 2007 (actual occupation)	21	
1 May 2007 to 31 May 2014		85
1 June 2014 to 30 November 2015 (last 18 months)	18	
	127	85

Exempt 127/212 × £120,000 = £71,887

4   Noddy is selling his main residence, which he has owned for 25 years. He lived in the house for the first 14 years of ownership, then for the next five years he was posted abroad by his employer. He never returned to live in the house during the remainder of his period of ownership.

What fraction of his gain will be exempt under the private residence exemption?

	✓
20.5/25	
14/25	
15.5/25	✓
19/25	

The five years posted abroad will not be deemed occupation as he never returned to live in the property. Therefore only the actual 14 years of occupation and the last 18 months of ownership will be exempt.

INDEX

Notes

Notes

Notes

Notes

Notes

Notes

Notes

REVIEW FORM

How have you used this Text?
(Tick one box only)

☐ Home study

☐ On a course_____

☐ Other _____

Why did you decide to purchase this Text? *(Tick one box only)*

☐ Have used BPP Texts in the past

☐ Recommendation by friend/colleague

☐ Recommendation by a college lecturer

☐ Saw advertising

☐ Other _____

During the past six months do you recall seeing/receiving either of the following?
(Tick as many boxes as are relevant)

☐ Our advertisement in Accounting Technician

☐ Our Publishing Catalogue

Which (if any) aspects of our advertising do you think are useful?
(Tick as many boxes as are relevant)

☐ Prices and publication dates of new editions

☐ Information on Text content

☐ Details of our free online offering

☐ None of the above

Your ratings, comments and suggestions would be appreciated on the following areas of this Text.

	Very useful	Useful	Not useful
Introductory section	☐	☐	☐
Quality of explanations	☐	☐	☐
How it works	☐	☐	☐
Chapter tasks	☐	☐	☐
Chapter overviews	☐	☐	☐
Test your learning	☐	☐	☐
Index	☐	☐	☐

	Excellent	Good	Adequate	Poor
Overall opinion of this Text	☐	☐	☐	☐

Do you intend to continue using BPP Products?   ☐ Yes   ☐ No

Please note any further comments and suggestions/errors on the reverse of this page. The Head of Programme of this edition can be emailed at: nisarahmed@bpp.com

Please return to: Nisar Ahmed, AAT Head of Programme, BPP Learning Media Ltd, FREEPOST, London, W12 8AA.

REVIEW FORM (continued)

TELL US WHAT YOU THINK

Please note any further comments and suggestions/errors below